COMPUTER

PROGRAMMING

JAVASCRIPT:

Table of Contents

Introduction

If there is anything, I want you to hold at the end of this programming guide for JavaScript is the fact that:

- JavaScript is the HTML and web language
- *It is easy to Learn*

If you can do that, then at the end, you will smile your way to programming for the web. However, your speed in learning JavaScript and other programming language is very dependent on you. If you find yourself struggling, don't feel demoralized rather take a break and reread the material after you have settled down. Remember, this chapter gives you the basics of JavaScript as a beginner to familiarize yourself with the language.

Variables in JavaScript

```
var exam = 50;

var test = 12;

var score = exam * test;
```

In the example above, exam, test, and score are variables given values with the value stored. We can perform various operations in JavaScript including multiplication, subtraction, addition, subtraction, and division. Variables and values can be declared as a number, string, or letter.

```
var name = "insert your name";

var number = '45';
```

From the example, you can enclose string with a single or double quote because they work exactly the same way.

JavaScript Identifiers

Every variable in JavaScript must have a unique name, which is used to identify it. These unique names are called identifiers. Identifiers have certain rules, which include:

- Every identifier must begin with a letter
- They can contain digits (0-9), letters (a-z), dollar signs ($), and underscores (_)
- Reserved words are not accepted
- Variable names are case sensitive

- *An identifier can begin with a dollar sign or underscore.*

Scope of JavaScript Variable

JavaScript allows two types of variable scope, which includes global and local variable scope. A variable is said to be global if it is declared outside the function body. With this, every statement has access to the variable within the same document. However, a local variable scope has its scope within the function. With this, the variable is only available to statements within the same function.

Basic JavaScript on the Browser side

When you hear about JavaScript on the browser side, it refers to the client-side, which means the code is run on the machine of the client – the browser. The browser-side components comprise of JavaScript, JavaScript libraries, CSS, images, HMTL, and whatever files downloaded to the browser.

Browser-Side JavaScript Features

JavaScript is important for the web as it is likely to use it to write programs that execute arbitrary computations. You have the opportunity of writing simple scripts such as the search for prime numbers or Fibonacci numbers. However, in the context of web browser and the Web, JavaScript enables programmers to program with the capability of computing sales tax, based on the information provided by the users through an HTML form.

The truth about JavaScript language is in the document-based objects and browser that the language is compatible with. This may sound complex, however, I will explain the significant capabilities of JavaScript on the browser side along with the objects it supports.

- *Controls the Browser* – There are various JavaScript objects that permit the control of the browser behavior. Furthermore, the Window object support means of popping up dialog boxes that display messages for the users. Additionally, users can also input messages. Besides this, JavaScript doesn't provide a method that gives users the opportunity to directly create and manipulate frames inside the browser window. Notwithstanding, you can take advantage of the ability to make HTML animatedly by creating the particular frame layout you want.

- *Interact with HTML Forms* – another significant part of the JavaScript on the browser side is its capability to work together with HTML forms. The ability comes because of the form element and its objects, which contains Text, submit, select, reset, radio, hidden, password, and text area objects. With these elements, you can write and read the values of the elements in the form.
- Interact with Users – *JavaScript has another feature, which is its ability to define event handlers. Most times, users initiate these events. For instance, when someone moves the mouse through a hyperlink, clicks the submit button, or enters a value. The capability to handle such events is important because programming with graphic interfaces requires an event-driven model.*

In addition to these aforementioned features, JavaScript on the browser side has other capabilities such as:

- Changing the displayed image by using the <img> tag to generate an animation effect and image rollover

- It has a window.setTimeout () method, which allows some block of random source code to be performed in the future within a split of a second
- It streamlines the procedure of working and computing with times and dates

JavaScript Framework

Take a moment and consider creating a web application and websites like constructing a house. In building a house, you can decide to create every material you need to start the house from scratch before building without any plans. This will be time-consuming and won't make much sense. One thing you may likely do is to buy pre-manufactured materials such as bricks, woods, countertops, etc. before assembling them based on the blueprint you have.

Coding is like taking it upon yourself to build a house. When you begin coding a website, you can code all areas of the site from scratch without. However, there are certain website features, which gives your website more sense by applying a template. Assuming you want to buy a wheel, it will make to look for one that you can reinvent. This is where JavaScript Frameworks come to the scene.

JavaScript Framework is a collection of JavaScript code libraries, which gives website developers pre-written JavaScript codes to use for their routine programming tasks and features.

You can also refer to it as an application framework, which is written in JavaScript where the developers can manipulate the functions of these codes and reuse them for their own convenience. They are more adaptable for website designing, which is why many developers use them in building websites.

Top JavaScript Framework

Vue.js

This is one of the JavaScript frameworks, which was created to make the user interface development more organized. Created by Evan You, it is the perfect JavaScript framework for beginners because it's quite easy to understand. Furthermore, it focuses on view layers. With Vue.js, you don't need Babel. A Babel is a transpiler with the responsibility of converting JavaScript codes to the old version of ES5 that can run in all browsers. All templates in the Vue.js framework are valid HTML, which makes their integration easier. If you want to develop lightweight apps as a beginner, it is best to start with Vue.js.

Next.js

Another important JavaScript Framework is the Next.js framework, which is an additional tool for server-side rendering. The framework allows developers to simplify the developing process similar to the Vue.js framework.

The features of this JavaScript Framework include page-based client-side routing and automatic splitting of codes. The framework also comes with a full CSS support, which makes styling of the user's interface easier for beginners and professionals.

Ember.js

This framework, which was created a few years ago, is among the most sought JavaScript framework in the web industry. Famous companies such as LinkedIn, Heroku, and Kickstarter use the Ember.js framework in the design of their websites. It also comes with regular updates and offers a complete feature for users. Unlike the Vue.js framework, it is effective for developers who want to develop complex web applications. The focus of this framework is on scalability, which allows developers to use it for both web and mobile projects.

Angular

Google released this JavaScript Framework in 2010 with regular updates and improvements taking place. It is one of the most sought after the framework for many developers because it simplifies the development of websites and apps. For other developers, it is because of its ability to create dynamic web apps.

Chapter 1. Use of a Global Variable as a Cache

In cases where a small app is to be created and in which one will incur an overhead when trying to integrate the app with a third-party mechanism, these can easily be handled inside the Node.js app, and this should be executed in the mode for a single thread.

In this mode, that is, the single threaded mode, a single application is executed at a time, and this is responsible for handling all of the requests sent to it. This is similar to what happens with desktop allocations. Other web apps developed by use of other programming languages for web development such as PHP, Ruby, and Python do not function in this manner. A global variable can be defined in this case, and this will become accessible to all of the requests that we make. This needs to be considered with a lot of concern.

For this mechanism to be achieved, one can create global variables of the necessary type and then a manipulation mechanism should be added inside this function. This will make it persist inside all of our requests.

Consider the code given below, which shows how this can be done effectively:

```
'use strict';

//this should be the cache for the js file

var  cache = {};

exports.someMethod = function(data){

/*The business logic should be added here*/

//setting the cache

cache[key] = val;

//retrieving the cache

cVal = cache[key];

//deleting the cache

delete cache[key];

/*The business logic should be added here*/
```

Logging without the use of a third-part Library

Whenever we want to print temporary information, we use the "*console.log*" so as to log in to the system. In the deployment stage, there are good libraries which can be used for this purpose. Some people hate the idea of using third-party libraries so as to log into their node.js app. However, this has been solved by the provision of an alternative. With the native support, one can be availed with a very decent mechanism for logging into their node.js app.

The Node.js's console object provides us with different levels of logging. These need to be used in the way they were designed to be used, otherwise, you will have trouble in using them. When you want to execute your node app, you should specify a logfile in which you will need to have everything written. This can be done as shown in the command given below:

$node app.js > mylogfile.log

After executing the above command, you will be set. The information about logging will be kept in the above file, and you will be in a position to view it later when you want to gain insight into some useful or critical information. It is also good for security purposes.

Whenever we want to print something on our console terminal, we should use the format given below:

console.log("The value of my variable should be:"+xyz);

This should only work for items which are single valued. If it was a json object, then we could have used "console.log(xyz)." This shows that the + operator does not work in this case.

About the use of "*"

It is recommended that this should not be used in a production dependency. Most people use it in their package.json file so as to specify the version or to use the "*" so that they can always have the latest package with them. One should have all of their packages updated to the latest version, since it might have some bug fixes, several improvements, and even new features added to it. However, this is only good for those whose product is in the development stage but has not reached the production stage.

In case of compatibility errors, fixing it will be easy. This is shown in the code given below:

```
//other of this:

"dependencies": {

"clustered-node": "*"

//use the following
```

```
"dependencies": {
```

```
"clustered-node": "~0.0.10"
```

For those who use such notations in a production environment, this is very risky. This is because one will not know when and which package might break and crash the application, which is possible. This is why it should only be used in the development phase, but once the product gets into the production environment, you should switch to dependencies which are based on a specific version. This should be done during the deployment phase of the product.

Asynchronous looping

Whenever we use the AsyncJS/underscoreJS in asynchronous flow looping/control, we get very useful and essential support. For those who know more about the callback concept, they can use it in a very native manner. If you are not interested in using this library in a simple task, then use the mechanism given in the code below. Here is the code:

```
var iterate = function(items, it){
```

```
console.log("Now handling: "+it);
```

```
//async methods
```

```
someAsyncMethod(parameterss, function callback(){

if(items.length <= it)return;

return iterate(items, ++it);

})

};

var items = [5, 6, 7, 8];

iterate(items, 0);
```

Chapter 2. The Basics of JavaScript Function and Scope

Let's see now, normally when we are talking about a 'function' what's the first thing that comes to your mind? Obviously an activity right?

The functions in JavaScript also work in a similar manner. Functions are blocks of codes which are required to be executed over and over again by the program. A Function is used to perform a particular task. A Function can contain any number of arguments and statements; they can even have none. Depending on how the structure is coded, it may or may not return any value to the user.

A Function is declared in the following manner:

Function name(   ) { /*code blocks to be executed*/}

To start the Function, we start with the function keyword, and then we add the *name,* and parentheses. To finish the function, we place the code blocks to be executed in a curvy brackets.

You can also put the function in a named variable-

```
var jam = function() {/* code blocks to be executed*/}
```

Below are few examples of how you can execute a function-

i) **This is the example of the most basic function**

```
varsayHello = function(person, greeting) {

var text = greeting + ' , '+ person;

console.log(text);

};

Say Hello (' Jessica' , ' Hello');
```

ii) **This is the example of a function that returns a value**

var greet = function (person, greeting)

{

var writing = greeting + ' , ' + person ;

return function () {console.log(text); };

}

console.log(greet('Richard' ,' Hello")));

iii) **Sometimes, you might want to use a nested function. (Note: A nested function is a function within another function.)**

varsayHi = function(person, greeting) {

var text = greeting + ',' + person;

return function() {console.log (text);}

};

var greeting = greet(' Richard' , 'Hello');
greeting();

Self-Executing Anonymous Function

Programmers have always been looking for the most advanced and clever methods available to improve their programming experience and ways to make it more accessible and easier for them. This resulted in the creation of the *Self-Executing Anonymous function*.

The core purpose of the self-executing anonymous function is to create a JavaScript function and then immediately execute it upon its conception.

This makes it much easier for a programmer who isworking on large scale programs. Likewise, it will help you to code without creating a messy global namespace.

A basic Self-Executing Anonymous Function Would be-

It is very important that you understand how to use this type of function if you plan on programming complex code in JavaScript. Using the Self-Executing Anonymous Function can produce some great code that is easy to use. As an example, the JQuery library is designed to make using JavaScript on websites much easier. It does this by wrapping the entire library in one large self-executing function.

Typeof Operator

You might run into a situation where you need to determine the type of variable that you are working in JavaScript. You won't have call Sherlock Holmes to find that! Instead, you can simply use the 'typeof' operator to determine the type of any specific value. In other words, the typeof operator is used to evaluate the type of the operand.

EX-

Varmyvar=0

alert(typeofmyvar) *//alerts "number"*

Number isn't the only type of operand that can be detected. It can also be: string, Boolean, object, null, and not defined.

Scope

Scope is the accessibility of a variable.
A good understanding of Scope is necessary when it comes to debugging because it allow you to know what variable from which code block is causing the problem.

The simple rule here is that whenever you declare a variable inside a scope, it will only be recognized by the statements that are inside that scope; the statements that are outside the scope will not acknowledge its existence and so that variable will not work.

Another way to look at this is to imagine your entire code as a hotel with specific functions and sections of code as hotel rooms. The hotel rooms represent the private scopes of the code, while the common areas represent the global scope. A person in one hotel room cannot see or use what is in another hotel room. Staff who work in the hotel (and the global scope) also don't have access to private hotel rooms unless they have specific permission. Meanwhile, guests can go through the common areas and make use of any object there.

Thus, you can see how scope can affect how your code runs. If you need two different functions to access the same variable, you need to ensure that they both have access to it. One key way to ensure that the necessary variables have access to is to make your variables globally accessible.

There are two possible alternatives if you want your variables to become globally accessible.

The first thing you can do is to declare the variable outside the scope of your given piece of code, this will allow any functions in your program to be able to call it and recognize it.

The other thing you can do is to declare the variables inside your scope without using the word var. If the same variable was not defined at the beginning of the code outside the scope of the piece of code in question, then the variable will act similarly to a global one.

Ex-

```
var foo = 'hello';

var talkHello = function() {

console.log(foo);

};
```

talkHello(); // logs 'hello'

console.log(foo); // also logs 'hello'

As you can see, the variable foo is declared outside of the function talkHello. That means that foo is a global variable and any function will be able to access it, so when the function talkHello calls it, it is accessible.

The following example is contradictory to the first example. This shows that a code block that was written outside the scope is not being able to recognize the variable.

```
var talkHello = function() {

var doo = 'hello';

console.log(doo);

};

talkHello(); // logs 'hello'

console.log(doo); // gives an empty log.
```

In this example, the variable doo is called inside the function talkHello. This creates a private variable that is only accessible to the function, hence when the command console.log(doo) attempts to access it, it returns a null value.

Some Common Mistakes to Avoid

☐ **Always remember that a variable is only accessible by the functions within a specific scope, outside of that scope the variable is invalid.**

Practice

☐ **Explain what a scope is and how the variables are affected by it.**

☐ **Write a simple program to illustrate the functionalities of a:-**

a) Simple Function

b) A Function with returnable value

c) A function passed as a parameter (Argument)

☐ Explain the concept of a Self-Executing Anonymous Function and give an example.

Chapter 3.   Loop Constructs

Looping is another fundamental programming construct that most programming languages support. Fundamentally, looping is used to execute the same set of statements iteratively until a condition remains true. JavaScript supports four types of looping constructs.

While Loop

The most basic loop construct is the while loop. This type of a loop executes the set of statements inside the while loop until the expression for the while is true. As soon as the expression becomes false, the while loop execution terminates. The syntax for implementation of while is given below –

while (expression){

//Statements of the while block

}

Sample implementation of the while loop is given below –

<html>

```
<body>

<script type="text/javascript">

<!--

var c = 0;

document.write("Loop begins...");

while (c < 5){

document.write("Value    of    c:    "    +    c    +    "<br
/>");

c++;

}

document.write("Loop Terminates!");

//-->

</script>

<p>Change the values of the looping variable to see
how things change</p>

</body>

</html>
```

The output of the code upon execution is shown in the image given below.

Do...While Loop

Another looping construct is the do...while loop. The condition's validity is checked at the end of the loop. So, this loop is that it executes at least once. This type of a loop executes the set of statements inside the do...while loop until the expression for the while is true. As soon as the expression becomes false, the while loop execution terminates. The syntax for implementation of while is given below –

do{

//Statements of the while block

}while (expression)

Sample implementation of the do...while loop is given below –

```
<html>

<body>

<script type="text/javascript">

<!--

var c = 0;

document.write("Loop begins...");

do{
```

```
document.write("Value of c: " + c + "<br
/>");

c++;

} while (c < 5)

document.write("Loop Terminates!");

//-->

</script>

<p>Change the values of the looping variable to see
how things change</p>

</body>

</html>
```

The output of the code upon execution is shown in the
image given below.

For Loop

The most commonly used looping construct is the 'for'
loop. The for loop integrates the looping variable
initialization, condition checking and looping variable
update in the for statement. The syntax for
implementation of while is given below –

```
for(init; expression; update){
```

```
//Statements of the for block

}
```

Here, init is the initialization statement and expression is the condition, which is to be tested. Lastly, the update is the expression that updates the looping variable. Sample implementation of the while loop is given below –

```html
<html>
<body>
<script type="text/javascript">
<!--
var c;
document.write("Loop begins...");
for(c=0; c<5; c++){
document.write("Value of c: " + c + "<br
/>");
}
document.write("Loop Terminates!");
//-->
</script>
```

<p>Change the values of the looping variable to see how things change</p>

</body>

</html>

The output of the code upon execution is shown in the image given below.

For...In Loop

This loop is typically used with objects. The loop uses a variable of the object and loops through until the value of the property associated with the object variable is exhausted. In other words, this loop works around object properties. The syntax for the implementation of the for...in loop is as follows –

for (variable in object){

//Statements inside the for...in loop block

}

Sample implementation to demonstrate the working of the for...in loop is given below.

<html>

<body>

```
<script type="text/javascript">

<!--

var demoObject;

document.write("Properties of the Object: <br />
");

for (demoObject in navigation) {

document.write(demoObject);

document.write("<br />");

}

document.write ("Loop Terminated!");

//-->

</script>

<p>Change the object to see how the result
changes</p>

</body>

</html>
```

Controlling the Loop

Although, once the loop starts, it terminates only when
the expression stated for condition holds false, there are

certain ways in which the developer can control the loop. There may be situation where you might want to terminate the loop in between execution if a special case occurs or you may want to start a new iteration on the occurrence of a scenario. In order to control and implement all these conditions, JavaScript has provided continue and break statements.

Break Statement

Whenever this keyword is encountered in a JavaScript code, the loop immediately terminates and execution is shifted to the statement that comes right after the closing bracket of the loop. In order to understand the working of break statement, let us take an example,

<html>

<body>

 <script type="text/javascript">

<!--

var a = 5;

document.write("Loop Begins...
 ");

while (a < 30)   {

if (a == 5){

```
break;

}

a = a + 1;

document.write( a + "<br />");

}

document.write("Loop terminates!<br /> ");

//-->

</script>

<p>Change the value of a to see how the loop execution
is modified</p>

</body>

</html>
```

The output of the code is shown in the image given below.

Continue Statement

When this statement is encountered in a loop, the rest of the loop statements are ignored and the control is shifted to the next iteration of the loop. With that said, it is important to understand that the next iteration is execution only if the loop condition is found true. In case, the loop expression is found false, loop execution is terminated.

The sample code given below demonstrates the use of continue statement.

```html
<html>

<body>

<script type="text/javascript">

<!--

var a = 0;

document.write("Loop begins<br /> ");

while (a < 9){

a = a + 1;

if (a == 4){

continue; // skip rest of the loop body

}

document.write( a + "<br />");

}

document.write("Loop terminates!<br /> ");

//-->
```

```
</script>
```

```
<p>Change the value of a to see how the result
changes!</p>
```

```
</body>
```

```
</html>
```

The output generated after execution of this code is illustrated in the image shown below.

Labels for Controlling Loop Flow

While the break and continue statements can redirect flow of control around the boundaries of the loop construct, they cannot be used to transfer control to precise statements. This is made possible in JavaScript with the use of labels. A label is simply an identifier followed by colon, which is placed before the statement or code block. The following code demonstrates the use of labels.

```
<html>
```

```
<body>
```

```
<script type="text/javascript">
```

```
<!--
```

```
document.write("Loop begins!<br /> ");
```

```
loop1: for (var i = 0; i < 3; i++) {

document.write("Loop1: " + i + "<br />");

loop2: for (var j = 0; j < 3; j++) {

if (j > 3 ) break ; // Quit the innermost loop

if (i == 2) break loop1; // Do the same thing

if (i == 4) break loop2; // Quit the outer loop

document.write("Loop2: " + j + " <br />");

}

}

document.write("Loop terminates!<br /> ");

//-->

</script>

</body>

</html>
```

The output of the code has been illustrated in the image given below.

Chapter 4.   An Introduction to ES6

Some of the key features of ES6 are:

Arrows - Arrows is a function shorthand using the '=>' syntax. It is syntactically similar to the related feature in C#, Java 8 and CoffeeScript.

Classes - There is support for classes, inheritance, super calls, instances and static methods.

Template strings - Template strings are used for constructing strings.

Modules - There is language-level support for component definition modules.

Data structures - There is support for Maps, Sets, WeakMaps and WeakSets.

Most modern browsers have support for ES6. If you want to try out ES6 code, there are a few online editors that can help you do so. Below are two of my favourites. Both of them provide the next generation of JavaScript compilers.

https://jsbin.com

https://babeljs.io/

Let's now look at some simple examples of ES6 JavaScript code. In these examples we are going to use JS Bin to enter and run the code.

Example 55: The following program is a simple example of ES6 scripting.

```
let num1=5;

        console.log(num1);
```

The following should be noted about the above program:

The 'let' command is used to assign values to variables.

We then output the value of the variable using the 'console.log' command.

With this program, the output is as follows:

5

We can also declare constants using the 'const' keyword. Let's look at an example of this.

Example 56: The next program is an example of ES6 scripting using constants.

```
const num=6;

let num1=5;

        console.log(num);

        console.log(num1);
```

With this program, the output is as follows:

6

5

We can also define functions in ES6. Let's look at a simple example.

<u>Example 57: The program below is an example of ES6 scripting using functions.</u>

```
var start=function()

        {
const num=6;

let num1=5;

        console.log(num);
        console.log(num1);
        }
        start();
```

With this program, the output is as follows:

6

5

Decision Making and Loops

ES6 has support for the following Decision Making and Loop commands.

If statement - This is used to evaluate an expression and then execute statements accordingly.

If...else statement - This is used to evaluate an expression and then execute statements accordingly. Then execute another set of statements if the Boolean expression evaluates to false.

Nested if statements - This is useful to test multiple conditions.

Switch...case statement - This evaluates an expression, matches the expression's value to a case clause, and executes the statements associated with that case.

For loop - Here a set of statements are executed 'n' number of times.

While loop - Here a set of statements are executed until a condition remains true.

Do...while loop - Here a set of statements are executed until a condition remains true. The difference from the while loop is that one execution of the statements will always occur.

Let's look at some examples of these statements.

Example 58: The following program is an example of loops (if else) in ES6.

```
var start=function()

        {
const num=6;

let num1=5;

  if(num<7){

console.log("The value is less than 7");}

  else{

console.log("The value is greater than 7");

  }

        }
        start();
```

With this program, the output is as follows:

"The value is less than 7"

Example 59: The next program is an example of loops (for loop) in ES6.

```
var start=function()
        {
  for(x=0;x<5;x++)
    {
      console.log(x);
    }
        }
        start();
```

With this program, the output is as follows:

0

1

2

3

4

Example 60: This program is an example of loops (while loop) in ES6.

```
var start=function()
        {
  let x=0;
  while(x<5)
    {
      console.log(x);
      x++;
    }
        }
        start();
```

With this program, the output is as follows:

0

1

2

3

4

Classes

ES6 also has the support for classes. A class can be defined as follows:

```
class classname

        {
        constructor(parameters)
        {
//Assign values to the properties

        }
// More methods

        }
```

Where:

'classname' is the name assigned to the class.

We have a constructor that is called when an object is created.

The constructor can take in parameters. These parameters can be used to assign values to the properties of the class.

We can then have more methods defined in the class.

Let's look at an example of a simple class in ES6.

Example 61: The following program shows how to use classes in ES6.

```
var start=function()
        {
  class Rectangle
    {
       constructor(height, width) {
      this.height = height;
      this.width = width;
    }
       Display()
       {
         console.log(this.height);
         console.log(this.width);
       }
    }
  var newrect=new Rectangle(3,4);
  newrect.Display();
        }
        start();
```

The following things can be noted about the above program:

First we define a class called 'Rectangle'.

It accepts 2 parameters, namely 'height' and 'width'.

This can be used to define the properties of 'height' and 'width' for the class.

We then create a 'Display' method that can be used to display the properties of the class.

With this program, the output is as follows:

3

4

Collections

ES6 also has the support for collections, such as the map collection. As an example, if we want to set the value of a map collection, we would use the 'set' method as shown below:

```
mapname.set(key,value);
```

Where:

- 'mapname' is the name of the map.

- 'key' is the key assigned to the element.

- 'value' is the value associated with that key.

Let's look at an example of using maps with ES6.

Example 62: The program below shows how to use maps in ES6.

```
var start=function()

    {
var map = new Map();

map.set('keyA','valueA');

map.set('keyB','valueB');

map.set('keyC','valueC');

console.log(map.get("keyB"));

    }
    start();
```

With this program, the output is as follows:

valueB

Chapter 5. Form

Form takes information from the web page visitors and sends it to a back-end application such as PHP script, CGI or ASP Script. HTML forms are used to collect data from visitors on a site. Forms are important for membership registration on a website, online shopping, or a job application form. For instance, during user registration, information such as email address, name, credit card, and so on would be collected. Then required processing would be performed on the sent data based on the specific logic contained in the back-end application. There are different available form elements such as the text area fields, radio buttons, drop-down menus, checkboxes, etc.

Form structure

<form>

HTML form is created with the <form> element. This tag must carry the action attribute at all times and would occasionally have an id and method attribute too.

Action

An action attribute is required for every <form> element. The value of the action attribute is the URL it contains for the page on the server which retrieves the information contained in the submitted form.

Method

Forms go to the back-end application in two ways. They "get" or "post".

Get

The GET method enables value from the form to return to the end of the specified URL in the action attribute. The GET method is perfect for data collection from the web server. The technique ensures parameter stores in the browser cache. There are limits of the quantity of information this method can send. Do not use the GET method while dealing with sensitive information such as passwords or credit card numbers because of the process that displays in the browser's address bar is visible to everyone.

Post

The POST method sends values through the HTTP headers. The POST method is perfect when the form contains sensitive information such as passwords and when visitors need to upload files. Parameters do not get saved in web server cache or browser history. The POST method is safer than the GET method.

Id

This value specifies a unique identity for an HTML form from other elements on the page.

Text input

The <input> tag enables the creation of different form controls. The type of attribute value determines the type of input created.

type="text"

With the type attribute value of the text, it creates a single line of text.

Name

When information is entered into a form by the user, the server demands to know what value the control data holds. For instance, in a login form, the server wants to know which declares the username and the password. Each form control needs the name attribute, and the attribute value recognizes the form control which is sent together with the information entered into the server.

Max length

The max length attribute can be used to determine the number of characters entered into a text field. The value of the max length attribute is the number of characters that it holds.

Password input

type="password"

The <input> tag of type "password" creates a way for users to input a password safely. The element presents a one-line plain text editor control replacing characters with a symbol such as the ("*") or a dot (" • ") which cannot be read and keeps the text secured.

Name

This attribute specifies the name of the password input which is transferred to the server including the password visitors enter.

<body>

<form action="http://www.alabiansolutions.com/login.php">

<p>Username:

<input type="text" name="username" size="15"maxlength="30" />

</p>

<p>Password:

```
<input type="password" name="password"
size="15"maxlength="30" />

</p>

</form>

</body>
```

Textarea

A multi-line input is created with the `<textarea>` element. The `<textarea>` is not an empty element compared to other input elements, therefore, it should contain an opening and closing tag. Texts that surface between the opening `<textarea>` and closing `</textarea>` elements will be displayed in the text box when the page is loaded.

```
<form action="process.php">

<p>What did you think of this gig? </p>

<textarea name="comment"></textarea>

</form>
```

Radio Button

The `<input type="radio">` element represents a radio button. It is used to create several selectable options.

Name

To be treated as a group, the value of the name attribute must correspond with the radio group because selecting any other radio button in the same group deselects the first selected button. A lot of radio groups can be created on a page as long as each has its name.

Value

The value attribute indicates the unique value connected with each selected option. Values of each button in a group should be different so the server can recognise the selected option.

Checked

The checked attribute specifies the selected value when the page loads. This attribute should be used by one radio button in a group.

```
<body>
```

Pizza Size:

```
<label>
```

```
<input type="radio" name="size"
value="small"/>Small</label>
```

```
<label>
```

```
<input type="radio" name="size"
value="medium"/>Medium

</label>

<label>

<input type="radio" name="size" value="large"/>Large

</label>

</body>
```

Checkbox

Checkbox is used to select and deselect one or more options.

type="checkbox"

Users are permitted to select or deselect one or more options in response to a question.

Name

This attribute is transferred to the server alongside the value of the option(s) selected by the user. The name attribute value must remain the same for all buttons when users have to respond to questions with options for answers in the checkboxes form.

Value

When a checkbox is checked, this attribute specifies the value sent to the server.

Checked

The checked attribute specifies the box that should be checked when the page is being loaded.

```
<body>

Pizza Toppings:

<label>

<input type="checkbox" value="bacon" />Bacon

</label>

<label>

<input type="checkbox" value="extra cheese" />Extra Cheese

</label>

<label>

<input type="checkbox" value="extra cheese" />Onion

</label>

</body>
```

Dropdown list box

A select Box, also known as the Drop-down list box enables the user to choose one option from a drop-down list. A drop-down list box is created with the <select> tag, and it consists of two or more <option> tags.

Name

The name attribute shows the form control name, which is being sent to the server together with the value selected by the user.

<option>

This element is used to indicate the options for a visitor. The text in-between the opening <option> and closing </option> elements will be displayed to the visitor in a drop-down box.

Value

The <option> tag utilises the value attribute to specify the value sent to the server together with the control name when the option is selected.

Selected

This attribute is used to specify the option that should be automatically selected when the page loads.

<body>

```html
<label>Phones:

<select name="devices">

    <option value="techno">Sony</option>

 <option value="infinix">Infinix</option>

    <option value="samsung">Samsung</option>

       <option   value="sony"   selected>Choose   a
device</option>

</select>

</label>

</body>
```

File input box

The file input box is used to enable users to upload a file on a web page. A file could be an image, audio, PDF or video.

type="file"

This input produces a box, a text input lookalike accompanied with a browse button. When the browse button is selected, a window pops up which enables users to select a file from their computer in order to be uploaded on the site.

```
<form action=" process.php" method="post">

<p>Upload your songs in MP3 format:</p>

<input type="file" name="user-song" /><br />

<input type="submit" value="Upload" />

</form>
```

type="submit"

This attribute is used when a user needs to submit a form.

```
<body>

<form action="process.php" method="post">

<p>Subscribe to our email list:</p>

<input type="text" name="email" value="email" />

<input type="submit" value="subscribe" />

</form>

</body>
```

Name

It can use a name attribute although it's not necessary.

Value

The value attribute is used to influence the appearance of the text on a button. It is advisable to designate the words that appear on a button because buttons default value on some browsers is "Submit query" and this can be inappropriate for forms.

Reset button

type="reset"

This button is used to erase all inputs by the user.

<input type="reset" value="Reset" />

Image button

An image can be used for the submit button. The type attribute must be given the value of the image. The SRC attribute can also be provided

<form

action="http://www.websitename.com/subscribe.php"

>

<p>Subscribe to our email list:</p>

<input type="text" name="email" />

<input type="image" src="subscribe.png" width="100" height="20"

alt="Subscribe" />

</form>

Button Tag

The <button> tag specifies a button that can be clicked. Texts, content, or images can be inserted into the <button> element. The buttons created with the <input> element is different from buttons created with the <button> tag. The <button> element attribute type should always be specified.

<button type="submit">Click Me! </button>

Fieldset Element

Longer forms benefit a lot from the <fieldset> element. It is used to group form controls that are related together.

<form method="post">

<fieldset>

    <legend>Contact Details</legend>

<label>Address:

      <input type="text" name="text">

    </label>

    <label>Phone Number:

```
<input type="number" name="number"><br>

     </label>

<label>Email:<br>

<input type="email" name="email"><br>

     </label>

</fieldset>

</form>
```

Legend element

The <legend> element appears immediately after the opening <fieldset> tag and consists of a caption which identifies the motive of that form control group.

```
<form method="post">

 <fieldset>

<legend>Contact Details</legend>

<label>Address:<br>

<input type="text" name="text"><br>

</label>

<label>Phone Number:<br>

<input type="number" name="number"><br>
```

```
</label>

<label>Email:<br>

        <input type="email"
name="email"><br>

</label>

 </fieldset>

</form>
```

Label element

The label tag can be used to caption a form control so that users would know what should be entered into the area.

```
<form >

      <label for="male">Male</label>

<input    type="radio"    name="gender"    id="male"
value="male"><br>

      <label for="female">Female</label>

 <input   type="radio"   name="gender"   id="female"
value="female"><br>

      <label for="other">Other</label>
```

```html
<input type="radio" name="gender" id="other" value="other"><br><br>

<input type="submit" value="Submit">

</form>
```

Chapter 6. Iframe and Multimedia

Iframe

The <iframe> element can be used to embed web pages into your web page.

Iframe embeds: Google Map

Google map can be embedded into your webpage using the iframe tag.

<iframe

src="https://www.google.com/maps/embed?pb=!1m1
8!1m12!1m3!1d3963.341775346873!

2d3.34222531484425853!3d6.604381995223933!2m3!
1f0!2f0!3f0!3m2!1i1024!2i768!4f1

3.1!3m3!1m2!1s0x103b8d7c33eb87b3%3A0xfc23c955
6f669273!2sWebsite+Name!5e0!3m2!1sen!2sng!4v151
6009132030" width="600" height="450"

frameborder="0"   style="border:0"
allowfullscreen></iframe>

Iframe embeds: YouTube

<body>

```
<iframe width="450" height="400"

src="https://www.youtube.com/embed/MhPGaOTiK0A"

frameborder="0" allowfullscreen></iframe>

</body>
```

Multimedia in HTML5

HTML5 enables users to embed video or audio using the native HTML tags. The browser will give users control to play the file if it supports it. Both audio and video tags are new features and can be used on the recent version of browsers. Popular video formats are .mp4, .m4v, Flash Video {.flv}, Audio Video Interleave {.avi} etc.

The video element:

A video player can be embedded using the video element for a specific video file. Those attributes are used to customize the player: preload, loop, auto play, poster, auto and controls.

Preload

The preload attribute instructs the browser on what action to take when the page loads. one of these three values can occur:

None: The video should not load automatically when the page loads until the user clicks play.

Auto: when the page loads the browser should download the video.

Metadata: this means that information such as first frame, size, track list and duration should be received by the browser.

Src

The path to the video is specified by this attribute.

Poster

This attribute enables users to direct an image to be displayed while the video downloads or until the user decides to play the video.

Width, height

The size of the player is specified with these attributes.

Controls

This attribute specifies that the browser should provide its own controls for playback when used.

Autoplay

This attribute indicates that the file should play automatically when used.

Loop

This attribute specifies that the video should start playing again from the beginning the moment it ends when utilized.

Multiple video formats

HTML5 enables users state multiple sources for audio and video elements so that browsers can use any one that works for them.

```
<video       poster="images/calvin.jpg"       controls
preload="none" width="450" height="420">

<source src="calvin.mp4" type="video/mp4" />

<source src="calvin.webm" type="video/webm" />

<source src="calvin.ogv" type="video/ogv" />

<p>Calvin Harris music video</p>

</video>
```

The audio element

Embedding an audio player into a page for a particular audio file is done using the audio element. Different attributes can be used to customize the player, attributes such as auto play, controls, loop and preload.

Autoplay

This is a boolean attribute. If utilized, the audio will play automatically and continue without stopping.

Loop

The loop attribute is also a boolean attribute, and it states that the audio will restart over and over again every time the audio ends.

```
<body>

<audio src="avicii.mp3" controls="true"
autobuffer="true"></audio>

</body>
```

Control

Audio controls are inserted using the control attribute, and it includes controls like pause, play, and volume. The <source> element enables the user to indicate alternative audio files that the browser could choose from. The browser would recognize the first organized format. Texts between the <audio> and </audio> elements will be displayed in browsers that do not recognize the <audio> element.

```
<audio src="audio/test-audio.ogg" controls autoplay>
```

```
<p>This browser does not support our audio format. </p>

</audio>
```

Multiple audio formats

```
<audio controls autoplay>

<source src="audio/test-audio.ogg" />

<source src="audio/test-audio.mp3" />

<p>This browser does not support our audio format. </p>

</audio>
```

Chapter 7.   The Document Object Model

The document object refers to your whole HTML page. After you load an object into the web browser, it immediately becomes a document object, which is the root element representing the html document. It comes with both properties and methods. The document object helps us add content to the web pages.

It is an object of the window, which means that having:

window.document

Is the same as having?

document

DOM Methods

DOM methods are the actions that you can perform on the html elements. The **DOM** properties are the values of the **HTML** elements which one can set or change. The following are the document object methods:

1. **write("string")**- it writes a string to a document.

2. **writeln("string")**- it writes a string to a document with a new line character.

3. **getElementById()**- gives the element with the specified id.

4. **getElementsByName()**-gives all the elements with the specified name.

5. **getElementsByTagName()**-gives all the elements with the specified tag name.

6. **getElementsByClassName()**-gives all the elements with the specified class name.

Accessing Field Values

The DOM is a good way of getting the values of an input field. Many are the times you will need to get input from a user. This can be done using the following property:

document.formname.name.value

Where:

- document- **is the html document representing our root element.**
- form name- **is the name of the form with the fields.**
- field name- **is the name of the input text.**
- **value**- is a property which returns the value of input text.

Consider the following example:

```html
<html>
<body>
<script type="text/javascript">
    function readValue(){
    var name=document.memberform.memberName.value;
    alert("Hi: "+name);
    }
</script>
<form name="memberform">
        Enter       Name:<input       type="text" name="memberName"/>
    <input    type="button"    onclick="readValue()" value="Click Here"/>
    </form>
</body>
</html>
```

When you run the code, it will give you the following simple form:

Just enter your name in the input field and click the Click Here button. See what happens.

You will get an alert box with your name and some text appended to it:

We simply created a simple form with an input text field. The method READVALUE() helps us get the value that we enter into the field. Consider the following line:

var

name=**document**.memberform.memberName.value;

The MEMBERNAME is the name given to the text field in the form, and these must match, otherwise, you will not the right results.

getElementById()

Other than the name, we can also get the element by its id. This can be done using the DOCUMENT.GETELEMENTBYID() method. However, the input text field should be given an id.

For example:

<html>

```
<body>

<script type="text/javascript">

    function computeSquare(){

    var x=document.getElementById("integer").value;

    alert(x * x);

    }

    </script>

    <form>

      Enter an Integer:<input type="text" id="integer"
name="myNumber"/><br/>

      <input type="button" value="Compute Square"
onclick="computeSquare()"/>

    </form>

</body>

</html>
```

The code should give you the following simple form upon execution:

Enter a number in the input field and click the Compute Square button.

This should return the square of the number in a popup box as shown below:

In the example, we have defined the COMPUTESQUARE() method which helps us get the square of a number entered in the input text field. Consider the following line:

var x=**document.**getElementById(*"integer"*).value;

In the line, we have used the GETELEMENTBYID() method which takes the id of the input text field as the argument. The method helps us get the value typed in the input text field using its id.

getElementsByName()

The DOCUMENT.GETELEMENTSBYNAME() method can help us get an element by its name. The method has the syntax given below:

document.getElementsByName(*"name"*)

The name is needed.

Example:

<html>

<body>

```
<script type="text/javascript">

    function getNumber()

    {

    var
    options=document.getElementsByName("option");

            alert("Total Options:"+options.length);

    }

    </script>

    <form>

        Yes:<input     type="radio"     name="option"
    value="yes">

        No:<input     type="radio"     name="option"
    value="no">

        <input   type="button"   onclick="getNumber()"
    value="Available Options">

</form>

</body>

</html>
```

Upon execution, the code returns the following:

Click the Available Options button and see what happens. A popup window will be shown as follows:

We have created two radio buttons with options YES and NO. Note that these two input types have been given the same name, that is, OPTION.

Consider the following line:

var options**=document.**getElementsByName(*"option"*)**;**

The line helps us count the number of elements with the name OPTION. This should be **2** as shown in the output.

getElementsByTagName()

The DOCUMENT.GETELEMENTSBYTAGNAME() property returns the elements with the tag name which is specified. It takes the syntax given below:

document.getElementsByTagName(*"name"*)

For example:

<html>

<body>

<script type=*"text/javascript"*>

function allparagraphs()**{**

```
var pgs=document.getElementsByTagName("p");

    alert("Total paragraphs are: "+pgs.length);
}
```

```
</script>

    <p>This is a paragraph</p>

    <p>This is a paragraph</p>

    <p>This is a paragraph</p>

    <p>This is a paragraph</p>

<button onclick="allparagraphs()">Total
Paragraphs</button>

</body>

</html>
```

The code returns the following upon execution:
Click the Total Paragraphs button and see what happens.
You will see the following popup:

This means that the code was able to count the number of paragraphs that we have.

The main logic lies in the following line:

```
var pgs=document.getElementsByTagName("p");
```

We have passed the tag **"p"** as the argument to our method, and the tag represents a paragraph. There are three elements with the tag **"p"**, so the output should be **4** paragraphs.

Here is another example:

< html>

<body>

<script type=*"text/javascript"*>

function countheader2**(){**

var

h2count**=document**.getElementsByTagName**(***"h2"***);**

    alert("Total count for h2 tags: "**+***h2count.length***);**

}

function countheader3**(){**

var

h3count**=document**.getElementsByTagName**(***"h3"***);**

    alert("Total count for h3 tags: "**+***h3count.length***);**

}

</script>

```
<h2>A h2 tag</h2>

<h2>A h2 tag</h2>

<h2>A h2 tag</h2>

<h2>A h2 tag</h2>

<h3>A h3 tag</h3>

<h3>A h3 tag</h3>

<h3>A h3 tag</h3>

<h3>A h3 tag</h3>

<h3>A h3 tag</h3>

<button         onclick="countheader2()">Total
h2</button>

<button         onclick="countheader3()">Total
h3</button>

</body>

</html>
```

The code returns the following output upon execution:

We have a total of **4 h2** tags and a total of **5 h3** tags. Click the Total **h2** button and see what happens.

You should get the following popup box:

Click the Total **h3** button and see what happens.

You should get the following popup box:

innerHTML

This property can be used for addition of a dynamic content to an html page. It is used on html pages when there is a need to generate a dynamic content like comment form, registration form, etc.

Consider the following example:

```
<html>

<body>

<script type="text/javascript" >

function displayform() {

        var data="Username:<br><input type='text'
        name='name'><br>Comment:<br><textarea
        rows='6'     cols='45'></textarea><br><input
        type='submit' value='Contact us'>";
document.getElementById('area').innerHTML=data;

 }

</script>

<form name="form1">
```

```
<input       type="button"       value="Contact       us"
onclick="displayform()">

<div id="area"></div>

</form>

</body>

</html>
```

The code returns the following button upon execution:

Click the button and see what happens. You will get the following:

What we have done is that we are creating a contact us form after the user has clicked a button. Note that the html form has been generated within a div that we have created and given it the name AREA. To identify the position, we have called the DOCUMENT.GETELEMENTBYID() method.

innerText

We can use this property to add a dynamic property into an HTML page. Note that when this property is used, your text is interpreted as a normal text rather than as html content. A good application of this is when you need to write the strength of a password based on its length, write a validation message etc.

For example:

```html
<html>

<body>

<script type="text/javascript" >

function validatePass() {

var message;

if(document.form1.userPass.value.length>5){

message="good";

}

else{

message="poor";

}

document.getElementById('area').innerText=message;

}

</script>

<form name="form1">
```

```
<input type="password" value="" name="userPass"
onkeyup="validatePass()">
```

Strength:`<span id="area">` Pasword strength `</span>`

`</form>`

`</body>`

`</html>`

The code returns the following upon execution:

Just begin to type the password and see what happens to the text on the right of the input field as you type. If you type less than 5 characters for the password, the message will change to poor as shown below:

Continue to type the password until you have more than 5 characters. You will see the message change to good as shown below:

That is how powerful this property is.

Animations

With JavaScript, we can animate elements. We can use JavaScript to move elements such as **<img />**, **<div>** etc. on a page depending on an equation. The following are the common methods used for animations in JavaScript:

1. setTimeout(method, time)- **this method will call the METHOD after someTIME in milliseconds.**
2. **setInterval (method, time)**- the method will call the METHOD after TIME milliseconds.

With JavaScript, one can set some attributes of the **DOM** object such its position on the screen. The position of the object can be set using TOP and LEFT attributes.

This is demonstrated below:

// Set the distance from the left edge of the screen.

object.style.left = distance measures **in** points or pixels;

or

// Set the distance from the top edge of screen.

object.style.**top** = distance measures **in** points or pixels;

Manual Animation

In the following example, we will be animating the image towards the right:

<html>

```
<body>

<script type="text/javascript">

        var image = null;

          function init(){

        image =
document.getElementById('myImage');

        image.style.position= 'relative';

        image.style.left = '0px';

        }

          function moveImage(){

        image.style.left = parseInt(image.style.left)
+ 10 + 'px';

        }

        window.onload =init;

    </script>

    </head>

  <body>

  <form>

  <img id="myImage" src="house.jpg" />
```

<p>Click the **button** to move the **image**</p>

`<input type="button" value="Move Image" `**`onclick=`**`"moveImage();" />`

</form>

</body>

</html>

You should use the correct name of your image in the following line:

`<img id="myImage" src="house.jpg" />`

In my case, I have a .jpg image named <u>HOUSE</u>. When I run the code, it returns the following:

Click the **"Move Image"** button. The image should move to the right with each click. This is shown below:

Consider the following line in the script:

image = document.**getElementById**(**'myImage'**);

We are getting the image using its **ID**, then it is assigned to the IMAGE variable. The INIT() method helps us set the initial position of the image on the window. The method will be called when the window is being loaded. The MOVEIMAGE() function will move the image towards the right by **10 pixels** after every click. To move the image towards the left, the value should be set as negative. The animation, in this case, is manual as we have to click a button.

Automated Animation

To automate the process of animating an element, we can use the SETTIMEOUT() function provided by JavaScript.

Example:

```
<script type="text/javascript">

        var image = null;

        var animate ;

        function init(){

                        image                  =
document.getElementById('myImage');

                image.style.position= 'relative';

                image.style.left = '0px';

        }

        function animateImage(){
```

```
        image.style.left = parseInt(image.style.left)
+ 10 + 'px';

        animate = setTimeout(animateImage,20);

    }

    function stopAnimation(){

        clearTimeout(animate);

        image.style.left = '0px';

    }

    window.onload =init;

  </script>

</head>

<body>

 <form>

    <img id="myImage" src="house.jpg " />

    <p>Click the Animate button to launch
animation</p>

        <input    type="button"    value="Animate"
onclick="animateImage();" />

        <input    type="button"    value="Stop"
onclick="stopAnimation();" />
```

</form>

The code returns the following upon execution:

Click the "Animate" **button. The animation should start. When you click the Stop button, the animation will stop.**

The ANIMATEIMAGE() method is calling the SETTIMEOUT method which sets the position of the image after every 20 milliseconds. This will result in the animation of the image. The STOPANIMATION() method helps in clearing the timer which is set by the SETTIMEOUT() method. The object, which is the image, is set back to its initial position.

Rollover

We can use a mouse image to rollover an image in JavaScript. Once you move the mouse over the image, it will change to another image.

Example:

<html>

<body>

<script type="text/javascript">

if(document.images){

```
        var img1 = new Image();

        img1.src = "ps.jpg";

        var img2 = new Image();

        img2.src = "house.jpg";

      }

    </script>

  </head>

  <body>

    <p>Move mouse over to rollover</p>

<a                                              href="#"
onMouseOver="document.img.src=img2.src;"

onMouseOut="document.img.src=img1.src;">

    <img name="img" src="nicsam.jpg" />

    </a>

</body>

</html>
```

We have used the IF statement to check whether the image exists or not. We have the used the IMAGE() constructor so as to preload some new object named

IMG1. The same has also been done to preload the second image, IMG2. The <u>SRC</u> is given the name of the image stored externally. The **#** helps to disable the link so that a URL is not opened once it is clicked. The method ONMOUSEOVER is called once the mouse cursor is moved over the image. The ONMOUSEOUT method will be called once the mouse cursor is moved out of the image.

Chapter 8. Clauses

GROUP BY clause

The GROUP BY clause gathers in all the rows that have data in the specified columns. It will also allow the aggregate functions we talked about earlier to be performed on the columns as well. The best way to explain this is with an example:

- SELECT column1,
- SUM(column2)
- FROM "list-of-tables"
- GROUP BY "column-list";

GROUP BY clause syntax:

Let's assume that you want to retrieve data on the maximum salaries paid for each separate department. Your statement would look like this:

- SELECT max(salary), dept.
- FROM employee
- GROUP BY dept;

This statement is going to show the highest salary in each unique department by name. In short, the name of the person in each department who earns the most will be displayed along with their salary and the department they work in.

HAVING clause

The HAVING clause is the one that lets you specify conditions on rows for each specific group, in other words, certain rows to be selected based on the specific conditions you input. The HAVING clause should always follow the GROUP BY clause if you are using it:

HAVING clause syntax:

- SELECT column1,
- SUM(column2)
- FROM "list-of-tables"
- GROUP BY "column-list"
- HAVING "condition";

The HAVING clause is best shown in an example so let's assume that you have a table that contains the names of your employees, the department they work in, their salary and their age. Let's say you want to find the average salary for each employee in each separate department, you would enter:

- **SELECT DEPT.,**
  AVG(SALARY)

- **FROM employee**
- **GROUP BY dept;**

But, let's now assume that you only want to calculate the average and display it if their salary is more than $20,000. Your statement would look like this:

- **SELECT DEPT, AVG(SALARY)**

- **FROM employee**
- **GROUP BY dept**

- **HAVING AVG(SALARY) > 20000;**

ORDER BY clause

The ORDER BY clause is optional and it lets you display your query results in an order that is sorted – either ascending or descending – based on whichever columns you choose to order the data by.

ORDER BY clause syntax:

- SELECT column1, SUM(column2) FROM "list-of-tables" ORDER BY "column-list" [ASC | DESC];

- [ ] = optional

This statement is going to show the employee ID, department, their name, age and salary from the table you specify – in this case, the employee_info table – where the department is equal to SALES. The results will be listed in ascending order, sorted by salary:

- <u>ASC = Ascending Order - default</u>
- <u>DESC = Descending Order</u>
- <u>For example:</u>
- <u>SELECT employee id, dept, name, age, salary FROM employee info WHERE dept = 'Sales' ORDER BY salary;</u>

If you want to order data from multiple columns, each column name must be separated with a comma:

- SELECT employee_id, dept, name, age, salary
- FROM employee_info
- WHERE dept = 'Sales'
- ORDER BY salary, age DESC;

Chapter 9. Operators, Data Types and Other Priorities

JavaScript Calculations

All programming languages allow you to perform calculations. You can use JS, in a sense, as a replacement pocket calculator. For example, enter the following:

```
"use strict";

console.log(3 + 4);
```

Listing 5 **accompanying_files/03/examples/calc.j s**

As expected, you get *7* as your result.

You can see a few key JS concepts just in this very small, simple example. *3 + 4* is an EXPRESSION. Expressions are one of the most important concepts in JS. Expressions characteristically have a RETURN VALUE — in this case, the number *7*.

In turn, you can use return values in different places in your code, e. g. as an argument to a function call. Or to put this another way, JavaScript replaces expressions by their (return) values.

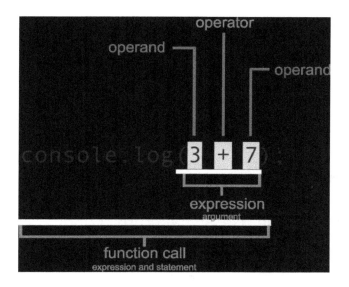

Expressions

Expressions in Firefox Web Console

You can also enter expressions directly into Firefox Web Console. Try entering *3 + 4* in the input line (next to the double arrow ") ().

Entering expressions directly in console — input

After you confirm your input with Return, the console will immediately display the return value ().

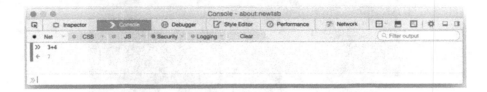

Entering expressions directly in console — output

FYI, you can also use Shift-Return to input a multi-line statement, i. e. a single statement which runs over multiple lines. The entire statement is executed only after you hit return.

Alternatively, you can also select parts of expressions in Scratchpad and examine these using **Inspect** (Ctrl-I / Cmd-I). As you see in , Scratchpad displays the result of *4 * 2* as *value: 8* in the side panel to the right.

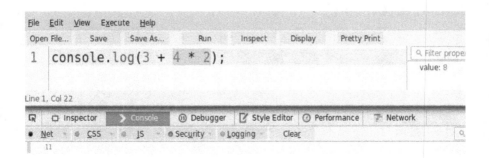

Inspect a selected (partial) expression in Scratchpad

Notation

From now on, we'll often point out a value returned by some expression or which appears at the console. To do this, we'll insert a comment in the code and show the value in front of a => — the so-called FAT ARROW.

Example

    3 + 4 // => 7

    console.log(3 + 4 * 2); //=> 11

JavaScript as a Pocket Calculator: Arithmetic Operators

In addition to multiplication and addition operators, JS has corresponding operators for the arithmetic operations of **subtraction**, **division** and **modulus**. All of these operators fall under the group of so-called ARITHMETIC OPERATORS:

Symbol	Operation
+	Addition
-	Subtraction
*	Multiplication
/	Division
%	Modulus — remainder of an integer division
**	Exponentiation (ECMAScript 2016+)

Table *Arithmetic operators*

Example

- *5 + 4* returns *9*

- *5 - 4* returns *1*

- *5 * 4* returns *20*

- *5 / 4* returns *1.25*

- *10 % 3* returns *1* since 10 - 3 * 3 = 1.

- *5 ** 4* returns *625* since 5 * 5 * 5 * 5 = 625 .

Exercise 3: 2000 Seconds

How many minutes and remainder seconds are there in 2000 seconds? Use *console.log* to print out the answer.

Tips: The easiest way to solve this exercise is to use the modulus operator. Right now, we haven't taught you how to remove decimal places; we'll come back to that later.

Characters and Strings

Have you noticed anything about how numbers and text are coded differently? The *"Hello world"* at the beginning of the previous lesson was written out in quotation marks, while numbers were not. A text element is written out within quotation marks, and actually involves stringing or linking individual characters together — giving us the programming term STRING to indicate such text.

Two Types of Quotation Marks

You may use both single quotes or double quotes to delimit a string, but the marks at the beginning and at the end of the string must be the same.

Example

"Some text string" is allowed

'Some text string' is also allowed

"Some text string' is invalid

Most JS developers consistently use double quotes, and only use single quotes in exceptional cases, e. g. when they need to use double quotes within a string to indicate literal wording.

Coding Guidelines

You should normally use double quotes to delimit strings.

Determining Length

Sometimes you need to know how long a string is — i. e. how many characters are in it. As you do more and more development, you'll come across many situations where length is important.

For example, blogs, lists of products, and similar items sometimes provide a text preview which only shows part of the entire text. Before generating this preview, the length of the entire text item must first be measured to see whether the text actually needs to be shortened.

So at this point, we'd like to introduce you to the string property LENGTH. You can have a string return this property by typing **.length** after the string.

"length matters - sometimes".length // => 26

Then pack your statement into a *console.log* so you can see the response you need on the console:

"use strict";

console.log("length matters - sometimes".length);

Listing 6 accompanying_files/03/examples/lengt h.js

Exercise 4: Lucky Numbers & Name Codes

Do you know about lucky numbers and code names? Here's an interesting way to come up with a name code:

Multiply the length of your first name (including your middle name(s) if you want) by the length of your last name and print out the result in the console. (Just to let you know, these are the numbers we got: 40 and 30.)

Literals: They Say What They Mean

Now that you've been introduced to strings and numbers, there's another important concept we need to tell you about: Basically, any value — whether a string or a number — which is specified literally in your code is known as a (you guessed it) *literal*. Literals always have a fixed value.

Examples

- 42

- "house"

- "green"

- 5.47

- 1998

- "Please enter your name"

Number & String Data Types

JavaScript literals have a so-called DATA TYPE. As the term implies, a data type specifies what kind of data the literal represents, and in turn its possible values.

Up to this point, we've used the following data types:

Data Type	Permissible Values / Meaning	Example of Literal
String	Any text	"Hello"
Number	Any positive or negative number	246.5

Table *String & number data types*

JavaScript encodes strings in so-called UTF-16 character format [ECMA-262]. An encoding format is responsible for how characters are represented digitally. UTF-16 makes it possible for you to use a wide variety of special characters as well as specific letters from different languages (e. g. German umlauts, accented French characters, etc.).

The value range for numbers is also limited. However, as long as you don't carry out any astronomical calculations, you should be safe.

It's easy to find out the data type of a literal — just use the JavaScript operator *typeof*. *typeof* returns a string which tells you the literal's data type.

Examples

```
"use strict";

console.log(typeof 3764);          // => number

console.log(typeof "beautiful JS"); // => string

console.log(typeof 27.31);          // => number
```

Listing 7 accompanying_files/03/examples/type. js

Exercise 5: Hmmm...So What are You Really?

What is the data type of the following literal?

"42"

Chapter 10. Document Object Model (DOM)

The document object is an object that is created by the browser for each new HTML page. When it is created, JavaScript allow us access to a number of properties and methods of this object that can affect the document in various ways, such as managing or changing information. As a matter of fact we have been continuously using a method of this object, document.write(), in order to display content in a web page. Nevertheless, before exploring properties and methods we will first take a look at the Document Object Model (DOM).

Fundamental DOM Concepts

We are aware that when the web browser receives an HTML file it displays it as a web page on the screen with all of the accompanying files like images and CSS styles. Nevertheless, the browser also creates a model of that web document based on its HTML structure. This means that all the tags, their attributes and the order in which they appear is remembered by the browser. This representation is called the Document Object Model (DOM) and it is used to provide information to JavaScript how to communicate with the web page elements. Additionally, the DOM provides tools which can be used to navigate or modify the HTML code.

The Document Object Model is a standard defined by the World Wide Web Consortium (W3C) that is used by most browser developers. To better understand the DOM, let us first take a look at a very simple web page:

```
<!doctype html>

<html>

<head>

<meta charset="utf-8">

<title>Party Schedule</title>

<style type="text/css">

.current {

color:red;

}

.finished {

color:green;
```

```
}
</style>
</head>
<body>
<h1 id="partytitle">Party Plan</h1>
<ul id="partyplan">
  <li id="phase1">20:00 - Home warm-up</li>
  <li id="phase2">22:00 - Joe's Bar</li>
  <li id="phase3">00:00 - Nightclub 54</li>
</ul>
</body>
</html>
```

On a web page, tags wrap around other tags. The <html> tag wraps around the <head> and <body> tags. The <head> tag wraps around tags such as <title>, <meta> and <script>. The <body> wraps around all content tags such as <p>, <h1> through <h6>, <ul>, <table> and so on.

This relationship between tags can be represented with a tree structure where the <html> tag acts as the root of the tree, while other tags represent different tree branch structures dependent on the tag hierarchy within the document. In addition to tags, a web browser also memorizes the attributes of the tag as well as the textual content within the tag. In the DOM each of these items, tags, attributes and text, are treated as individual units which are called nodes.

Image 26. Tree structure of an HTML document

In the tree structure for our basic HTML page the <html> element acts as a root element, while the <head> and <body> elements are nodes. In defining this relationship we can also refer to <html> as the parent node, and the <head> and <body> elements as child notes. In turn, both the <head> and <body> elements contain child nodes and so on. When we reach an item that contains no other child node we terminate the tree structure at that node, also known as a leaf node.

Selecting Document Elements

With the DOM structure in place, JavaScript can access the elements within the document in several different ways, dependent on whether we want to select individual or multiple elements. In all approaches we first have to locate the node representing the element we need to access and subsequently use the content, child elements and attributes of that node.

Selecting Individual Elements

To select individual elements we most commonly use the getElementById() method. This method will let us select an element with a particular ID attribute applied to its HTML tag. This method is the most efficient way to access an element if we follow the presumption that the ID attribute is unique for every element within the page. In the following example we will access the element whose ID attribute has the value 'phase1':

var firststop = document.getElementById("phase1");

By using the getElementById() method on the document object means that we are searching for the element with this ID anywhere on the page. Once the 'phase1' element is assessed, which in our case is the first <h1> element, the reference to this node is stored in the firststop variable and we can use JavaScript to make changes. As an example we will assign the attribute class with the value 'current' to this element. We will include this code in a <script> tag in the <head> section of our document.

```
var firststop = document.getElementById("phase1");

firststop.className = "current";
```

Image 27. Changing the style of a page element

> *Note:* In some browsers we have to either put the <script> tag before the closing </body> tag or in an external .js file in order for the code in this chapter to work.

If we want to collect the text from a node, we can use the textContent property. More importantly, we can also use the textContent property to change the content of the node. In the following example we will first select the element that has the value 'partytitle' in its id attribute and assign it to the title variable. Then we will effectively change the text of this element by changing the textContent property of the title variable. Let us add the following lines to our JavaScript code:

```
var title = document.getElementById("partytitle");

title.textContent = "Party Schedule";
```

Image 28. Changing the content of a page element

Selecting Group Elements

While sometimes selecting an individual element will be sufficient, other times we may need to select a group of elements. For example, we might need to select all <li> tags on a page, or all elements that share a class attribute. In these cases JavaScript offers the following two methods:

- *getElementsByTagName()* – a method which will let us select every instance of a particular tag.
- *getElementsByClassName( )* – a method that retrieves all elements that share a particular class name.

Selecting a group of elements means that the method will return more than one node. This collection of nodes is known as a NodeList and will be stored in an array-like item. Each node will be given an index number, starting with 0, while the order of the nodes will be the same order in which they appear on the page. Although NodeLists look like arrays and behave like arrays, semantically they are a type of object called a collection. As an object, a collection has its own properties and methods which are rather useful when dealing with a NodeList.

The following example will select all <li> elements and assign their node references to the schedule variable.

```
var schedule = document.getElementsByTagName("li");
```

If we want to access each element separately, we can use an array syntax. For example:

```
var item1 = schedule[0];
```

```
var item2 = schedule[1];
```

```
var item3 = schedule[2];
```

However, when we select a group of items we usually want to interact with the whole group. As an example, let us assign the class attribute with the "finished" value to all <li> elements. For this purpose we can use a loop to go through each element in the NodeList.

```
var schedule =
document.getElementsByTagName("li");
for (var i = 0; i < schedule.length; i++) {
schedule[i].className = "finished";
}
```

Image 29. Changing the class attribute for all <li> elements

Similarly to working with arrays, when working with collections we can use the length property to determine the size of the collection. We can then use this information in a for loop in order to effectively go through every NodeList item and assign the "finished" class attribute.

We can use exactly the same logic for the getElementsByClassName() method. We will get a NodeList stored in a collection with each node having an index number. Like with the getElementByTagName() method, we can access individual items and manage the collection through its object properties and methods.

Traveling Through the DOM

When we use any of the previously discussed methods to select an element node, we can also select other elements in relation to this elements. This type of relative selection is considered as an element property.

previousSibling & nextSibling

The previousSibling and nextSibling properties refer to adjacent elements on the same DOM level. For example, if we select the second <li> element with the id value "phase2", the "phase1" <li> element would be considered a previousSibling, while the "phase3" <li> element would be nextSibling. In the case where there is no sibling, (ex. the "phase1" element has no previousSibling), the value of this property remains null.

In the following example we select the <li> element which has "phase2" as a value for its id attribute and we change the class attribute for both the selected element and its previous sibling.

```
var secondstop = document.getElementById("phase2");

var prevstop=secondstop.previousSibling;

secondstop.className = "current";

prevstop.className = "finished";
```

Parents & Children

We can also travel to different levels of the DOM hierarchy using the selected element as a starting point. If we want to move one level up we can use the parentNode property. For example, if we have the second <li> element selected we can refer to its parent element, the <ul> element, with the following syntax:

```
var secondstop = document.getElementById("phase2");

var upperelement = secondstop.parentNode;
```

Alternatively, if we want to move one level down, we can use either the firstChild or the lastChild property. In the following example we have selected the <ul> element with "partyplan" as a value for its id attribute. Using the firstChild property we refer to the first <li> element of this list, while with the lastChild property we refer to the last <li> element of this list.

```
var plan = document.getElementById("partyplan");

var child1 = plan.firstChild;

var child2 = plan.lastChild;
```

Adding and Managing Content

Until this point we discussed how to find elements in the DOM. The more interesting aspect are the approaches to managing content within the DOM.

Changing HTML

We already talked about the textContent property, but this property retrieves only text values and ignores the subsequent HTML structure. If we want to edit the page HTML we have to use the innerHTML property. This property can be used on any element node and it is capable of both retrieving and editing content.

```
var liContent =
document.getElementById("phase1").innerHTML;
```

When retrieving the HTML from the <li> element with "phase1" as a value for its id attribute, innerHTML captures the whole content of the element, text and markup, as a string variable. If we apply the same syntax for the <ul> element, the innerHTML property will capture all of the <li> items.

We can also use the innerHTML property to change the content of the element. If this content contains additional markup, these new elements will be processed and added to the DOM tree. For example, let us add the <em> tag to the first <li> item in the party list:

var firstStop = document.getElementById("phase1");

firstStop.innerHTML = "<em>20:00 - Home warm-up</em>";

Image 30. Adding an <em> element with content to the first list item

DOM Manipulation

A more direct technique to managing document content is to use DOM manipulation. This is a 3-step process that uses the following methods:

1. *createElement()* - The process begins by creating a new element node with the createElement() method. This element node is

stored in a variable and it is not yet a part of the DOM.

2. *createTextNode()* - The process continues by creating a new text node with the createTextNode() method. Like in the previous step, this text node is stored in a variable and it is not a part of the document.

3. *appendChild()* - The final step is adding the created element to the DOM tree with the appendChild() method. The element will be added as a child to an existing element. The same method can be used to add the text node to the element node.

As an example let us create a new element that we will add to the existing party list. We will use the createElement() method and add this element to the newPlan variable.

```
var newPlan = document.createElement("li");
```

Following, we will create a new text node and add its content as a value to the newPlanText variable.

```
var newPlanText = document.createTextNode("04:00 - Back to home");
```

We can now assign the content of the text node to the newPlan element by using the appendChild() method.

newPlan.appendChild(newPlanText);

Finally, we would like to add this element to the list. We will use the getElementById() method to select the list through its "partyplan" id, and apply the appendChild() method to attach the newPlan element to the list.

document.getElementById("partyplan").appendChild(n ewPlan);

The complete syntax is as follows:

var newPlan = document.createElement("li");

var newPlanText = document.createTextNode("04:00 - Back to home");
newPlan.appendChild(newPlanText);
document.getElementById("partyplan").appendChild(n ewPlan);

Image 31. Adding a new <li> element

Using a similar process we can also use DOM manipulation to remove an element from the page. As an example let us remove the <h1> element which acts as the main page heading. We will first select the element through its id attribute with "partytitle" as its value and store that element node in a variable.

var removeHeading = document.getElementById("partytitle");

Next, we will need to find the parent element which acts as a container for the <h1> element, which in this case is the <body> element. We can either select this element directly, or use the parentNode property of the previously selected element. In either case we will need to store the parent element in another variable.

var containerForHeading = removeHeading.parendNode;

Finally, we will use the removeChild() method on the parent element in order to discard the element that we want removed from the page.

containerForHeading.removeChild(removeHeading);

The complete syntax is as follows:

var removeHeading = document.getElementById("partytitle");

var containerForHeading = removeHeading.parentNode;

containerForHeading.removeChild(removeHeadin g);

Image 32. Removed heading

Chapter 11. Events (Not the Kind You Celebrate)

If you can finish the new chat feature by tonight, we'll throw an office party to celebrate its release. Nothing fancy, just some drinks, good music and a little something to eat …

The chat code is now stored in a separate JavaScript file and is also a little cleaner. But Marty's not completely happy, there's still something missing...

Of course, visitors to the website shouldn't have to program JS to highlight chat members — highlighting should change automatically based on the input in the search box.

In order for that to happen, the code needs to react to user input. Your browser provides so-called EVENTS for just that purpose (no, we don't mean events like weddings or parties — unfortunately).

Browser Events

Any exertion of influence by a user, no matter how small, is considered by your browser to be an event. An event can be almost anything, including:

- clicking on a button

- moving your mouse over an image

- releasing an input key

- leaving an input field using your mouse or by tabbing

- finger gestures on a touch screen, e. g. zoom

There're also events which aren't triggered directly by users, and are triggered instead through occurrences like network requests or files which have finished loading. But first, we'll concentrate only on those events directly related to user behavior.

Dealing With Events as They Come Up: Event Handlers

Preliminary Measures

First, try a small experiment in your console. The event you're interested in is a user releasing a key while typing in an input field. Look in the chat HTML document and you'll find the input field (INPUT element) within a DIV element with the ID member_search:

<div
id
member_search

```
<input
type
text
placeholder
...Find a member...
/>
</div>
```

First, let's select the field using $('#MEMBER SEARCH INPUT'). You'll get back the INPUT element as a return value in the console. Move your cursor over the element in the console and you'll see that it's the right field.

Now, we'll bind an event to that field. To do this, we'll use the method ADDEVENTLISTENER. That method is available on almost every HTML element object.

$('#member search input').addEventListener(...);

ADDEVENTLISTENER requires two arguments. The first argument is the EVENT TYPE, in the form of a string. The event type we should use in this case is 'KEYUP', or releasing a key.

$('#member search input').addEventListener('keyup', ...);

ADDEVENTLISTENER's second argument must be a function — this will be executed by your browser when the specified event occurs. In this case, we'll just use a simple function to make sure the process is working:

() => alert(1)

FYI, the function you register on an event is called an EVENT LISTENER or EVENT HANDLER, and it's responsible for processing the event you specify.

And now our statement is complete — let's test it out in the console:

$('#member_search input').addEventListener('keyup', () => alert(1));

If you go to the member search input box and type in a character, an alert box with the alert 1 will appear as soon as you release the key. Of course, this function isn't very useful yet. And maybe clicking away alert boxes is making you a little irritated — but at least now you know how event handlers work. Mission accomplished!

Putting Everything Together

Now comes the tough part — you need to combine your existing code for highlighting and for event registration into one complete program.

Delete the call HIGHTLIGHTCHATMEMBERS('ERT'); from your JS file. Instead, your KEYUP event should now trigger the function call:

$('#member_search_input')

  .addEventListener('keyup', () =>

   hightlightChatMembers('ert'));

And actually, as soon as you type a key in the search box, the highlighting changes. However, instead of permanently highlighting the string 'ERT', we want to use the actual input. But how can we do that?

Once again, we'll need to use the input element object. We can retrieve it by using the selector $('#MEMBER_SEARCH_INPUT'), then query it for the value input by the user. We'll find that value in the property VALUE, i. e. $('#MEMBER_SEARCH INPUT').VALUE. You'll learn more about VALUE and other properties in **lesson 6**.

Putting it all together, we get the following statement:

```
$('#member_search input')
    .addEventListener('keyup', () =>
        hightlightChatMembers($('#member_search input').value));
```

Which then gives us the following overall code:

```
1
"use strict";
2

3

4
    const highlightChatMembersBy = partOfMemberName => {
5
        chatMembers()
6
            .filter(member =>
7
```

```
        doesMemberMatch(partOfMemberName,
member))

 8

        .forEach(highlight);

 9

 };

10

11

 const   doesMemberMatch  =  (partOfMemberName,
memberElement) =>

12

   memberElement.innerHTML.toLowerCase()

13

        .includes(partOfMemberName.toLowerCase());

14

15

 const chatMembers = () => $$("#chat_members li");

16

 const highlight = el => el.classList.add("highlighted");
```

```
17

18

  const $ = document.querySelector.bind(document);

19

  const                    $$                    =
document.querySelectorAll.bind(document);

20

  NodeList.prototype.  proto  = Array.prototype;

21

22

  $("#member_search_input")

23

    .addEventListener("keyup", () =>

24

    highlightChatMembersBy($("#member_search
input").value));

25
```

Listing 16 accompanying_files/05/examples/highlight_c
hat_members_1_event/highlight_chat_members.js

Enter different strings and experiment a little with your current implementation. What do you notice?

Guard Clauses: Protection for Your Functions

Oops — I just found a bug. If I search for a chat member, suddenly all of them are highlighted.

Could you fix that? As it is, we can't possibly put the highlight feature online.

Okay, here's the problem — although the program is highlighting the matching members, it's not removing that highlighting again when the search string is updated.

Instead of going through the trouble to find out what highlighting we need to remove, it'd be a lot simpler just to remove all highlighting, then highlight only those chat members who match the search. To do this, we'll need some additional code which removes the corresponding CSS class from all members:

```
const removeHighlightsFromAllChatMembers = () =>
  chatMembers().forEach(removeHighlight);
const removeHighlight = el =>
el.classList.remove('highlighted');
```

FYI, it's not a problem that a few <u>LI</u> elements with chat members don't have the class *highlighted* at all — in that case, nothing will be removed.

Order the two functions according to their level of detail. In addition, we still need to add a call to the new function <u>REMOVEHIGHLIGHTSFROMALLCHATMEMBERS</u>. To do this, we recommend you create a higher-level function called <u>UPDATEHIGHLIGHTINGOFCHATMEMBERS</u>, which first removes all highlights (<u>REMOVEHIGHLIGHTSFROMALLCHATMEMBERS</u>) then marks the matching chat members (<u>HIGHTLIGHTCHATMEMBERSBY</u>):

<u>const updateHighlightingOfChatMembers = partOfMemberName => {</u>

<u> removeHighlightsFromAllChatMembers();</u>

<u> hightlightChatMembersBy(partOfMemberName);</u>

<u>};</u>

Now we just need to add the new function <u>UPDATEHIGHLIGHTINGOFCHATMEMBERS</u> to the event handler in place of the function <u>HIGHTLIGHTCHATMEMBERSBY</u>, which was only responsible for highlighting. We then get the following code:

1

```
"use strict";
```

2

3

4

```
const   updateHighlightingOfChatMembers   =
partOfMemberName => {
```

5

```
  removeHighlightsFromAllChatMembers();
```

6

```
  highlightChatMembersBy(partOfMemberName);
```

7

```
};
```

8

9

```
const removeHighlightsFromAllChatMembers = () =>
```

10

```
     chatMembers().forEach(removeHighlight);

11

12

 const highlightChatMembersBy = partOfMemberName
=> {

13

   chatMembers()

14

     .filter(member =>

15

       doesMemberMatch(partOfMemberName,
member))

16

     .forEach(highlight);

17

 };

18

19
```

```
  const  doesMemberMatch  =  (partOfMemberName,
memberElement) =>
```

20

```
   memberElement.innerHTML.toLowerCase()
```

21

```
    .includes(partOfMemberName.toLowerCase());
```

22

23

```
  const chatMembers = () => $$("#chat_members li");
```

24

```
  const highlight = el => el.classList.add("highlighted");
```

25

```
  const     removeHighlight      =      el      =>
el.classList.remove("highlighted");
```

26

27

```
  const $ = document.querySelector.bind(document);
```

28

```
const                    $$                =
document.querySelectorAll.bind(document);
```

29

```
NodeList.prototype.  proto  = Array.prototype;
```

30

31

```
$("#member search input")
```

32

```
    .addEventListener("keyup", () =>
```

33

```
updateHighlightingOfChatMembers($("#member searc
h input").value));
```

34

Listing 17 accompanying_files/05/examples/highlight_c
hat_members_2_remove/highlight_chat_members.js

The code from **listing 17** works … almost. It works
except for the small glitch that all members are selected
in case of blank input. But the empty string occurs in
every string!

We can suppress this behavior just by adding code at the beginning of the function HIGHTLIGHTCHATMEMBERSBY to check whether PARTOFMEMBERNAME is empty. In case of an empty string, the function just needs to refuse to work. Add a RETURN to make the function exit prematurely.

```
if (partOfMemberName === "") return;
```

Code like this, which runs before the main body of a function is actually executed to make sure the values of the arguments passed to the function make sense, are called guard clausesor just GUARDS. They protect functions from invalid input values.

```
const hightlightChatMembersBy = partOfMemberName => {

  if (partOfMemberName === "") return;

  chatMembers()

    .filter(member                                 =>
doesMemberMatch(partOfMemberName, member))

    .forEach(highlight);
};
```

Listing 18 The function highlightChatMembersBy with a guard

The code from **listing 18** finally behaves like it should. But before you run to Marty to bring him the good news, let's take a little time to add a couple of improvements. Your maintenance programmer will thank you for that someday!

Making a Stunning Entrance Using init

The event registration code is still just kind of out there, with no motivation — it would be better to put it into its own function. This will give us a number of advantages — the code will be reusable and it'll also have its own name, making it easier to identify. In addition, putting the code into a separate function will provide us advantages in terms of things we haven't yet covered in this class — e. g. the code will be easier to test.

A good function name might be *registerEvents*, or even just *init*. If we wanted to, we could get even more specific and name the function *registerEventsForChatMemberHighlighting*. However, given the context (i. e. our entire file is geared for a specific task) the generic *init* is perfectly acceptable.

The name *init* stands for initialization. It's a function which calls all other functions, acting as an entry point into the rest of the code in the program. We could essentially name the function anything we wanted to, but *init* has already been established as the name for such functions. Other programmers can read the function name and understand immediately what we mean by it.

Based on our newspaper metaphor, INIT's function definition belongs at the beginning of your code. However, the call to INIT() can be made only after all other function have been defined.

1

"use strict";

2

3

4

```
const init = () => $("#member_search_input")
```

5

```
.addEventListener("keyup", () =>
```

6

```
   updateHighlightingOfChatMembers($("#member_searc
h_input").value));

7

8

   const        updateHighlightingOfChatMembers        =
partOfMemberName => {

9

   removeHighlightsFromAllChatMembers();

10

   hightlightChatMembersBy(partOfMemberName);

11

   };

12

13

   const removeHighlightsFromAllChatMembers = () =>

14

   chatMembers().forEach(removeHighlight);

15
```

```
16

  const hightlightChatMembersBy = partOfMemberName
=> {

17

   if (partOfMemberName === "") return;

18

   chatMembers()

19

     .filter(member =>

20

       doesMemberMatch(partOfMemberName,
member))

21

     .forEach(highlight);

22

 };

23

24
```

```
  const doesMemberMatch = (partOfMemberName,
memberElement) =>
```

25

```
  memberElement.innerHTML.toLowerCase()
```

26

```
     .includes(partOfMemberName.toLowerCase());
```

27

28

```
  const chatMembers = () => $$("#chat members li");
```

29

```
  const highlight = el => el.classList.add("highlighted");
```

30

```
  const removeHighlight = el =>
el.classList.remove("highlighted");
```

31

32

```
  const $ = document.querySelector.bind(document);
```

33

```
 const                    $$              =
document.querySelectorAll.bind(document);

34

 NodeList.prototype.   proto   = Array.prototype;

35

36

 init();

37
```

Listing 19 accompanying_files/05/examples/highlight_c hat_members_3_init/highlight_chat_members.js

Take a Look Behind the Facade With the Event Object

The fact that our current code can use some improvements will become clear once we take a closer look at event registration.

```
$('#member_search_input')
  .addEventListener('keyup', () =>
   hightlightChatMembers($('#member_search_input').value));
```

The function we'll register as our event handler here is:

```
()   =>   hightlightChatMembers($('#member search
input').value);
```

The interesting thing to note here is that the function, when it's called by the event, is automatically passed the event as an argument. So we just need to implement a parameter to capture the event:

```
event => hightlightChatMembers($('#member search
input').value);
```

What can we do with the EVENT? One thing would be to print it out to the console to see what it contains:

```
event => {

  console.log(event);

  hightlightChatMembers($('#member search
input').value);
```

If you type the letter **a**, the console will show:

```
keyup  {  target:  <input>,  key:  "a",  charCode:  0,
keyCode: 65 }
```

If you click on *keyup*, you'll see that EVENT is a JS object of "type"[1]KEYBOARDEVENT. Keyboard events have a number of very interesting properties — the table below shows you just a few:

1 In reality, JS doesn't have specific object types. It would be more correct to say that *keyup* is a JS object which has the KEYBOARDEVENT object in its prototype chain. We're using the term *type* here for purposes of simplification. It's only to show that all objects of the same "type" also have the same properties.

Property	Content
type	keyup
code	KeyA
key	a
timeStamp	[timestamp, i. e. when the event occurred]
target	[element which triggered the event]
ctrlKey	false [was the Ctrl key pressed?]
altKey	false [was the Alt key pressed?]

Events have many other properties, but just the few we've listed above show you that an event object contains all the information which comes into play when an event occurs, e. g.:

- What type of event is it? *keyup*

- What key was released? *a*

- When was the event triggered?

- From where was the event triggered?

Your event handler can then put this information to use. TARGET is the property which is of primary interest to us in our current program. TARGET contains the input field we intend to use, which we'd otherwise select by using $('#MEMBER SEARCH INPUT'). Therefore, we could also register our event handler as follows:

event => hightlightChatMembers(event.target.value);

Doing so gives us a number of concrete advantages. In all cases, it's more efficient, since your browser doesn't have to find the element object again — it's already in TARGET. But a much more important advantage is better maintainability. If our selector for finding the input field should change (e. g. because of a change to the HTML structure), we won't have to worry about also changing the event handler. It always refers to the current TARGET, no matter how we found the element and registered the event on it.

1

```
"use strict";

2

3

4

  const init = () => $("#member_search_input")

5

    .addEventListener("keyup", event =>

6


updateHighlightingOfChatMembers(event.target.value))
;

7

8

  const      updateHighlightingOfChatMembers      =
partOfMemberName => {

9

    removeHighlightsFromAllChatMembers();

10

    hightlightChatMembersBy(partOfMemberName);
```

11

```
};
```

12

13

```
const removeHighlightsFromAllChatMembers = () =>
```

14

```
  chatMembers().forEach(removeHighlight);
```

15

16

```
const hightlightChatMembersBy = partOfMemberName
=> {
```

17

```
  if (partOfMemberName === "") return;
```

18

```
  chatMembers()
```

19

```
    .filter(member =>
```

20

```
      doesMemberMatch(partOfMemberName,
member))
21
      .forEach(highlight);
22
  };
23
24
  const doesMemberMatch = (partOfMemberName,
memberElement) =>
25
    memberElement.innerHTML.toLowerCase()
26
      .includes(partOfMemberName.toLowerCase());
27
28
  const chatMembers = () => $$("#chat_members li");
29
  const highlight = el => el.classList.add("highlighted");
```

30

```
const       removeHighlight       =       el       =>
el.classList.remove("highlighted");
```

31

32

```
const $ = document.querySelector.bind(document);
```

33

```
const                $$                =
document.querySelectorAll.bind(document);
```

34

```
NodeList.prototype.__proto__ = Array.prototype;
```

35

36

```
init();
```

37

Listing 20 accompanying_files/05/examples/highlight_c
hat_members_4_target/highlight_chat_members.js

FYI, we can abbreviate EVENT as E. Normally
abbreviations are considered "bad" and should be
avoided, but in this case it's okay. The single letter E is

a common abbreviation for <u>EVENT</u> and is acceptable as long as its scope (range over which a variable exists) is limited to a very small function.

Now we're ready! You can finally show Marty the improved feature, and he's so happy about it he throws another party — here's to hoping it'll be an unforgettable event!

Chapter 12. A Storing Information in Variables

Learning to use Variables

In this chapter we are going to discuss variables. Variables are important elements of any programming language, and Javascript is no exception.

Variables are memory allocations used to hold values. They are called variables because their value may vary over time throughout the execution of the program.

You can use variables to hold text values (also known as alphabetic or string values) such as a person's name, company name or any other text content in your program. Variables may also hold numerical values.

To show you how variables are used, let's start with an HTML document page. For this example, we will use an HTML 4.01 document. To insert Javascript, a script tag is used with attributes set as follows:

<script language="javascript" type="text/javascript">

All Javascript commands must be placed within the script element. The first Javascript element that must be identified is the variable to be used. We need to name the variable and declare it.

When you declare a variable in Javascript, you use the *var* statement followed by the name of the variable. It is ideal that the name of the variable is something that describes what the variable represents. The variable name can be any alphanumeric set of characters, and should be treated as case sensitive. No punctuation marks or special characters are allowed, except for underscore.

An example of a variable declaration is:

var userName;

It's not required to use the var statement when declaring a variable in Javascript, however, it is a good idea always to do so. Consistently using var when declaring variables avoids difficulties with variable scope.

We'll be discussing variable scope later in the course, but the short explanation is that there are variables that are only used within a certain segment of your program, such as a function. Variables can be declared so that their value is only retrievable within that scope.

Now that we have declared our variable, we can assign it a value. This is called *variable assignment*. When we set the initial value of the variable, it is known as *initialization*. Once you have declared your variable, you no longer need to use the var statement. All you need is the name of the variable followed by the equal sign and the value of the variable. In this example, our variable initialization is:

userName="Mark Lassoff";

The value assigned in the above example is a string, also known as text, which is why it was enclosed with quotes. If you are assigning a numerical value to a variable, you do not need to enclose the value with quotes. For example:

age = 39;

A shortcut method for simultaneously declaring and initializing variables is to combine declaration and initialization on the same line. This is a more efficient way of initializing and declaring a variable. Declaring and initializing a variableConcurrently is as follows:

var userName="Mark Lassoff";

We can now display the variable's value. To display the value of the variable you can use the *document.write()* command, followed by the name of the variable in parentheses. The command syntax is:

document.write(userName);

When you want to display the variable's value, you do not need to put quotes around the variable name (like you would if you were outputting text). Instead you simply write the variable name in the parentheses. If it is the actual string value you want to print, then surrounding the string value with quotes is a must. For example:

document.write ("Austin, Texas");

This will display Austin, Texas.

We can also change the value of a variable during the program's execution. Suppose you have displayed the first value assigned to your variable. You then assign another value to the same variable name and then have it displayed. The second value assigned to *userName* replaces the initial value.

So far, we have been assigning values to our variable with the equal sign. However, the equal sign does not mean "equal to" in the context of Javascript. In Javascript, the equal sign is known as the *assignment operator*. The assignment operator merely assigns a value to the variable.

We will discuss more operators and their functions in greater detail later on. The way we read the variable initialization in the previous example is that the variable *userName* was assigned the value Mark Lassoff. The value being in quotes indicates it as a string value.

When a number is assigned as the value of a variable, it is referred to as a *numeric variable*. This is an example of declaring and assigning a numeric variable:

var userAge= 37;

In the next section, we will use numeric variables to perform some arithmetic operations.

The complete example code listing for the above discussion is presented here, followed by a screenshot of the expected output when viewed in the browser.

Code Listing: Declaring and Assigning Variables
<!DOCTYPE HTML PUBLIC "-//W3C//DTD HTML 4.01//EN"

"http://www.w3.org/TR/html4/strict.dtd" >

```html
<html lang="en">

<head>

</head>

<body>

  <script language="javascript"

      type="text/javascript">

    //var userName="Mark Lassoff";

    var userName;              //Variable Declaration

        userName="Mark     Lassoff";        //Variables
Initialization

            document.write(userName);              //No
quotes:  Output value of variables

        userName="Brett  Lassoff"; // = Known  as  the
assignment operator

      document.write("<br/>");

      document.write(userName);

      document.write("<br/>");

        var    userAge    =    37;        //Combined
initialization/declaration

        document.write(userAge);
```

```
</script>

</body>

</html>
```

This is how the output appears in the browser. Notice how the names and age were displayed on separate lines. This was made possible by using the break *
* tags, along with the *document.write()* command.

Questions for Review

1. In Javascript, what statement do you use to declare a variable?

a. variable

b. declare

c. var

d. dar

2. What happens if you don't put quotes around a variable's string assigned value?

a. The script outputs the value of the variable.

b. You get an HTML error.

c. The script will not assign the variable correctly.

d. Nothing will happen.

3. Which of the following is known as the assignment operator in Javascript?

a. The + sign

b. The = sign

c. The – sign

d. The @ sign

4. Which is an example of combined initialization/declaration?

a. var Size

b. Size = 0

c. var Size; Size = 0;

d. var Size = 0;

5. Why is it important to use the var statement every time you declare a variable?

a. You will have trouble with variable scope if you don't.

b. Variables won't work without being declared.

c. It's confusing without it.

d. You shouldn't use it.

Lab Activity

1) Create a Javascript code that will display the following output:

2) The program must have two variables. The first variable will hold the values for the adult animals, *adultAnimalName*, while the second variable will hold the values for the young animal, *youngAnimalName.*

3) Assign one value to each of the variables. Have these two variable values displayed using *document.write()*.

4) Use the following values for your program:

adultAnimalName	youngAnimalName
Horse	Pony
Goat	Kid
Dog	Puppy

```html
<!DOCTYPE HTML PUBLIC "-//W3C//DTD HTML
4.01//EN"

"http://www.w3.org/TR/html4/strict.dtd"

  >

<html lang="en">

<head>

</head>

<body>

  <script language="javascript"
type="text/javascript">

    var adultAnimalName;

    var youngAnimalName;

    adultAnimalName = "Horse";

    youngAnimalName = "Pony";

    document.write(adultAnimalName);

        document.write(":");

    document.write(youngAnimalName);

    document.write("<br/>");
```

```javascript
adultAnimalName = "Goat";

youngAnimalName = "Kid";

document.write(adultAnimalName);

    document.write(":");

document.write(youngAnimalName);

document.write("<br/>");

adultAnimalName = "Dog";

youngAnimalName = "Puppy";

document.write(adultAnimalName);

    document.write(":");

document.write(youngAnimalName);

document.write("<br/>");
    </script>
</body>
</html>
```

Variable Operators

In this section we are going to discuss variable operators. Once again, start with an HTML 4.01 file, and make sure you include a <script> tag to indicate to the browser that we are using Javascript.

First, we need to declare two variables as *operandOne* and *operandTwo*. These two variables will be assigned the values 125 and 15.371, respectively.

Note that they are two distinct value types. The variable *operandOne* holds the *integer number* 125, while the variable *operandTwo* contains the *floating point number* 15.371. A floating point number is capable of holding numbers with decimal points.

operandOne = 125;

operandTwo = 15.371;

In other programming languages, you would normally have to declare the specific variable type—you have to tell the program if you are using an integer or a floating point number. However, Javascript automatically understands what variable type you are creating the moment you assign its value. There is no need to explicitly specify which type of variable you are using.

With our variables defined and initialized, we can have them displayed as output using the *document.write()* command. Since you are instructing that the program's output be whatever the variable contains, you do not need quotation marks. Let us display the two values on two different lines. The code should be written as follows:

```
document.write (operandOne);

document.write ("<br/>");

document.write (operandTwo);
```

We can also perform arithmetic operations with our variables. To add the two numbers together, we use the addition operator "+". If we want the sum of the two variables displayed, then our code should be:

```
document.write("The sum is " + (operandOne + operandTwo));
```

The addition operator is used twice in this example. The plus (+) sign has two purposes in Javascript—it can be used as a *string concatenation operator,* and also as an *addition operator*. When we write *operandOne + operandTwo*, we are using it to add the two variables.

Concatenation, on the other hand, is also an important operation in any programming language. In Javascript, concatenation joins two strings or values together. In the context of this example, we are concatenating (placing next to each other) the string value "The sum is" to the sum of the two variables. The addition operation is placed within its own parentheses so the program understands that it is a separate operation from the concatenation.

Here is a list of the variable operators you can use and how they function:

Operator	Symbol	**Function**
Addition	+	Adds variables together and concatenates strings and other values.
Subtraction	-	Subtracts the value of one variable from another.
Multiplication	*	Multiplies variables.
Division	/	Divides one variable from another.

Modulus	%	Outputs the remainder of the division operation.
Increment	++	Adds one to the value of the variable.
Decrement	--	Subtracts one from the value of the variable.

The increment and decrement operators function by increasing and decreasing, respectively, the value of the variable by one.

There are two ways to use the increment and decrement operators. When the operator is placed after the variable, it is called a *postfix operator*. This means that the mathematical expression is evaluated and then the increment takes place.

The following code listing provides examples on how each variable operator is used.

Code Listing: Variable Operators

```
<!DOCTYPE    HTML    PUBLIC    "-//W3C//DTD    HTML
4.01//EN"

    "http://www.w3.org/TR/html4/strict.dtd"

    >

<html lang="en">

<head>

</head>

<body>

    <script language="javascript"
type="text/javascript">

        var operandOne;

        var operandTwo;

        operandOne = 125;        //Integer

        operandTwo = 15.371;    //Floating Point Number

        document.write(operandOne);

        document.write("<br/>");

        document.write(operandTwo);

        document.write("<br/>");
```

```
document.write("Addition " + (operandOne +
operandTwo));

document.write("<br/>");

document.write("Subtraction " + (operandOne -
operandTwo));

document.write("<br/>");

document.write("Multiplication " + (operandOne *
operandTwo));

document.write("<br/>");

document.write("Division " +
(operandOne/operandTwo));

document.write("<br/>");

document.write("10 % 3 " + (10 % 3));

document.write("<br/>");

document.write("11 % 3 " + (11 % 3));

operandOne++;     //Increment Operator Add One
to the variable;

operandTwo--;     //Decrementing One from the
variable

document.write("<br/>");
```

```javascript
document.write(operandOne);

document.write("<br/>");

document.write(operandTwo);
/*

    variable++   <--- PostFix Increment Operator

    ++variable   <--- PreFix Increment Operator

    PostFix-  The  rest  of  the  mathematical
expression is evaluated and then

    the increment takes place

    PreFix-  The increment takes place and then the
rest of the expression

    is evaluated

    */
var teamCity;

var teamName;

teamCity ="New York";

teamName= "Yankees";

var fullTeamInfo = teamCity + " " + teamName;

document.write("<br/>");
```

```
    document.write(fullTeamInfo);

  </script>

</body>

</html>
```

In order to better understand how concatenation works, an example of concatenating two string variables and outputting them is demonstrated within the previous code. We have created a new variable called *fullTeamInfo* and concatenated the two variables *teamCity* and *teamName*. We also concatenated a space within the quotation marks so the two variable strings are spaced properly. The output "New York Yankees" is the result.

This is a screenshot of the output shown in the browser. Here all possible use of concatenation is shown; all four mathematical operations are also demonstrated including the modulus operator.

Questions for Review

1. What does the "+" symbol mean when you place it next to a numerical variable?

a. Add the values together.

b. Take away the values.

c. Concatenate the values.

d. Divide the values.

2. What does the "+" symbol mean when you place it between two string values?

a. Add the values together.

b. Take away the values.

c. Concatenate the values.

d. Divide the values.

3. What does the % operator do?

a. Gives you the sum of division.

b. Gives you the remainder after division.

c. Gives you the multiplication sum.

d. Gives you the subtraction sum.

4. Which is the increment operator?

a. −

b. *

c. ++

d. #

5. How does a prefix increment operator function?

a. It adds one to the variable.

b. The rest of the mathematical expression is evaluated and the increment takes place.

c. It subtracts one from the variable.

d. The increment takes place and then the rest of the expression is evaluated.

1) Create an HTML 4.01 document. In the document body, add script tags with the appropriate attributes to add Javascript code.

2) Declare the following variables (but do not initialize yet):

     firstName
     lastName
     age
     city
     favoriteFood

3) Initialize the variables with information about you. (Your first name, last name, age, etc.)

4) Create a variable called *operand1* and use combined initialization and assignment to assign it an initial value of 1555.

5) Create a variable called *operand2* and use combined initialization and assignment to assign it an initial value of 96.255.

6) Demonstrate your knowledge of the mathematical operators with *operand1* and *operand2* by adding, subtracting, multiplying, and dividing the two values. Format your output as follows:

1555 + 96.255 = 1651.255

The line of code that would produce this output is:

document.write(*operand1* + " + " + *operand2* + " = " + (*operand1*+*operand2*));

7) Demonstrate the use of increment operator with *operand1* and decrement operators with *operand2*. Display the results.

```
<!DOCTYPE    HTML    PUBLIC    "-//W3C//DTD    HTML
4.01//EN"

    "http://www.w3.org/TR/html4/strict.dtd"

    >

<html lang="en">

<head>

</head>

<body>

    <script language="javascript"
type="text/javascript">

        var firstName;

        var lastName;

        var age;

        var city;

        var favoriteFood;
```

173

```javascript
firstName = "Bob";

lastName = "Smith";

age = 45;

city = "Boston";

favoriteFood = "Continental";

var operand1 = 1555;

var operand2 = 96.255;

document.write(operand1 +" + "+operand2 + "="
+ (operand1 + operand2));

document.write("<br/>");

document.write(operand1 +" - "+operand2 + "="
+ (operand1 - operand2));

document.write("<br/>");

document.write(operand1 +" x "+operand2 + "="
+ (operand1 * operand2));

document.write("<br/>");

document.write(operand1 +" / "+operand2 + "="
+ (operand1 / operand2));

document.write("<br/>");
```

```
    document.write("After increment, " + operand1 +
" is now ");

    operand1++;

    document.write(operand1);

    document.write("<br/>");

    document.write("After decrement, " + operand2 +
" is now ");

    operand2--;

    document.write(operand2);

    document.write("<br/>");

    /* Since there were no instructions to display the
values of the first five variables that were asked to be
declared and assigned, they will not be seen in the
output */

    </script>

</body>

</html>
```

In this chapter we learned about variables, their declaration, initialization, and combined initialization/declaration. You also learned how to output variables.

We also discussed operators, which included the assignment operator and arithmetic operators. You learned that the plus sign (+) can be used as an addition operator or concatenation operator and also learned how to concatenate strings and variables.

Chapter 13. JavaScript Essentials

Since this chapter is quite dense, here's an overview of what you can expect to learn:

1. Data types - how JavaScript classifies information. This is important because knowing what type of information you have will also tell you what you can do with that information (e.g., you can't multiply 5 with apples.)

2. Comparison Operators - lets you compare certain types of information (e.g., is 5 less than 10?). This is useful when you want to give the computer instructions that relies on certain conditions being met (e.g., allow the user to register only if the age is more than or equal to 18)

3. Console.log() - lets you display the output of a single line of code - useful when you want to see how information flows in your program per line of code.

4. Flow Control - if-else statements give the computer different instructions to execute depending on which condition is met (e.g., allow the user to enter site if the age is more than 18, otherwise, display an error message)

5. Debugging - when your program behaves erratically (e.g., misspelling the user's name or forgetting it completely), then you need to find which part of your code is messing up your program's behavior - this process is called debugging. This can become rather daunting when the code spans more than a thousand lines - knowing where to look will come in handy.

So far, you've played with strings and numbers using JavaScript. In the programming world, these categories of information are referred to as data types.

Data Types

Data types simply tell the computer how your information should be read. For instance, if you type the following into the console:

```
"5" + "5"
```

You'd get "55." This is because by enclosing 5 using quotation marks, you're telling the interpreter that you want 5 to be treated as a string, not a number. The addition operator, then, instead of adding the two numbers, combines the two strings. Now try removing the quotation marks and notice how the output changes to 10. There are different things you can do with different data types, so it's extremely important to know which one to use:

1. Strings - Anything you enclose in quotation marks will end up being a string. This can be a combination of letters, spaces, numbers, punctuation marks, and other symbols. Without strings, you wouldn't be able to get the user's name, address, email, and other important details.

2. Numbers - Self-explanatory; numbers are the ones you can perform addition, subtraction, multiplication, and division to, among other mathematical operations. Remember not to put quotation marks or you'll turn them into strings!

So far, we now have strings and numbers at our disposal, but remember the console output when you've tried playing with confirmation dialogues? Whenever you press OK, the console returns true, and whenever you press CANCEL, the console returns false. These outputs aren't surrounded by quotation marks, but they surely aren't numbers, so what in the world are they?

3. Booleans - booleans are data types that can only be either true or false. This is different from a string or a number, because it helps the computer make decisions based on whether or not certain conditions are met. For example, if you want to prevent minors from registering in your site, you'd have to have some sort of code to separate minors from the adults, like:

```
var age = 17

age >= 18
```

The console, then, returns false because the age is under 18. Now try the following mathematical expressions out and see what you get:

```
5 > 10
```

```
6 < 12
```

The first line should return false, while the second line should return true.

Comparison Operators

So far, we've talked about three data types (numbers, strings, and booleans), as well as some basic mathematical operators (+, -, *, /). What you've just used to test out booleans, however, are comparison operators (<, >, =), which are extremely important in managing the flow of your program. Here's the complete list and what they can do:

> Greater than

< Less than

>= Greater than or equal to

<= Less than or equal to

== Equal to

!= Not equal to

To test out these operators, replace the '@' symbol with the correct operator in the following statements in order to make the console output true:

```
console.log(5 @ 1);

console.log(1 @ 5);

console.log(5 @ 2);

console.log(1 @ 6);

console.log(5 @ 5);

console.log(10 @ 5);
```

Knowing what the Interpreter is Thinking

Notice how the JavaScript interpreter only gives you the latest output of the commands you type in, so if you've typed in three lines of code that should have different outputs:

```
5 > 10

6 < 12

7 > 14
```

Executing them all at the same time in the console, you'd only get the result of the last line (false).

You can, instead, enter each line of code individually so you can see the output of each command, but this gets especially tedious in larger bits of code. When you get to more complicated stuff, you'll eventually run into more errors and bugs. When this happens, you'll want to know what happens in specific commands you give so that you can pinpoint exactly where things go wrong.

console.log() takes whatever code you put inside and logs its execution to the console. That being said, let's see console.log() in action:

```
console.log(5 > 10)

console.log(6 < 12)

console.log(7 > 14)
```

Now you can see the output of each line of code!

Flow Control

You now know the most basic data types, mathematical operators, comparison operators, and a couple of neat console tricks. In order to make them useful, however, we need to be able to manipulate the flow of commands. For instance, if you wanted to create a user registration form that asks for the user's name, email address, age, and password, you'd first declare the variables as:

```
var name;

var email;

var age;

var password;
```

Now we'd need to store the user's input. For now, we use the prompt function:

```
name = prompt('What's your name?');

email = prompt('What's your email?');

age = prompt('What's your age?');

password = prompt('Please enter your desired password: ');
```

Assuming you've entered the right kind of information in the data fields, the name, email, age, and password variables now have the right type of data to process and store. What if, however, the user leaves the email field blank, or the age field with a letter? We can't just let the program continue if some of the vital fields of information don't have the right kind of data, therefore we use flow control statements. The first one we shall discuss is the if statement.

If Statement

If you've already programmed before, the structure of an if statement in JavaScript should be almost identical to the one you're familiar with:

```
if (<condition>)
{
    <action>
}
```

If you haven't already programmed before, an if-statement basically tells the computer to do whatever is inside the curly brackets ({}) if the if condition is true. If we want to, for instance, prevent the user from entering a blank field, we can do the following:

```
name = prompt('What's your name?');

if (name.length == 0)

{

    name = prompt('You cannot leave this empty.
What's your name?');

}

email = prompt('What's your email?');

if (email.length == 0)

{

    email = prompt('You cannot leave this empty.
What's your email address?');

}

age = prompt('What's your age?');

if (age.length == 0)

{

    age = prompt('You cannot leave this empty. What's
your age?');

}

password = prompt('Please enter your desired
password: ');

if (password.length == 0)

{

    password = prompt('You cannot leave this empty.
Please enter your desired password:');

}
```

The code can seem overwhelming for the first-time programmer, but when you read each line carefully, you'll see that they follow quite a neat and logical structure:

1)   First, since the prompt() function gives you whatever the user types in, you store the string inside a variable so you can use it later in the program.

2)   The if statements check if the variable is empty by checking if the length is equal to zero or not.

A)   IF THE LENGTH IS EQUAL TO ZERO, IT ASKS FOR INPUT AGAIN.

B)   IF THE LENGTH ISN'T EQUAL TO ZERO, IT DOESN'T ASK FOR INPUT AGAIN.

Take note that this sample code only serves to illustrate how the if statement works. Under no circumstances should you keep using the prompt() function to ask the user for information.

Now, what if you want to do something else in case your first condition isn't met? For instance, what if you want to say "Your name is <name>. Got it!" after the user types in a valid name? Then we add an else condition, followed by a second pair of curly braces that enclose the second set of commands:

```
name = prompt('What's your name?');

if (name.length == 0)

{

    name = prompt('You cannot leave this empty.
What's your name?');

}

else

{

    alert('Your name is ' + name + '. Got it!');

}

email = prompt('What's your email?');

if (email.length == 0)

{

    email = prompt('You cannot leave this empty.
What's your email address?');

}
```

```
else

{

    alert('Your email is ' + email + '. Got it!');

}

age = prompt('What's your age?');

if (age.length == 0)

{

    age = prompt('You cannot leave this empty. What's
your age?');

}

else

{

    alert('Your age is ' + age + '. Got it!');

}

password  =  prompt('Please  enter  your  desired
password: ');

if (password.length == 0)

{
```

```
    password = prompt('You cannot leave this empty.
Please enter your desired password:');

}

else

{

    alert('Your password is ' + password + '. Got it!');

}
```

Now your code sounds a little more human, as it responds better to user input. Try messing around with the code and see how the interpreter changes the output depending on the conditions met with the if-else statements.

Debugging

So far, you've managed to play around with variables, data types, mathematical operators, comparison operators, user prompts, confirmation dialogues, and alerts, and lastly, if-else statements. Don't worry if you make a couple of mistakes; computers are intrinsically literal and will not tolerate the tiniest syntactical mistakes. That being said, here are a couple of codes that don't seem to work as intended. Change the following code snippets so that you can produce the appropriate output!

```
var name = "Chris";

alert('Hi ' + 'name' + '! It's nice to meet you.');
```

In this code snippet, the output is supposed to be "Hi Chris! It's nice to meet you." What's the current output and what do you think is wrong with the code? Notice that the console doesn't complain and throw you an error message when you execute this code. This kind of problem is called a 'bug,' because while the JavaScript interpreter sees nothing wrong with this code, it doesn't work as the creator intended.

Now try to correct this code snippet that contains both bugs and errors:

```
var name;

var age;

name = prompt('What's your name?');

if (name.length = 0);

{
```

```
    name = prompt('You cannot leave this empty.
What's your name?');

}

else (name.length != 0)

{

    alert('Your name is ' + name + '. Got it!');

}

age = prompt('What's your age?');

if (age.length = 0)

{

    age = prompt('You cannot leave this empty. What's
your age?');

}

else (name.length != 0)

{

    alert('Your age is ' + age + '. Got it!');

}
```

This code is a distorted version of a previous sample code, so you may try to compare the codes and see why this one doesn't work. If you feel stuck, you can check out a program called 'linter,' which is a handy tool that checks your code for errors and tells you which lines have them. It's good exercise to practice your debugging skills now, because when you create more complex programs, debugging becomes almost routine.

What to look for when debugging:

Looking for bugs and errors can be quite overwhelming if you don't know where to look. Here are some of the most common mistakes programmers make when coding:

1. Using '=' instead of '==' to compare two values - the '=' sign in programming is used as an assignment operator, which means that if you use this instead of the '==' sign, you end up replacing the value of the variable on the left hand side of the equation with the value on the right hand side of the equation.

2. Misplacing the semicolon - just as periods end sentences in the English language, semicolons end statements in JavaScript, as well as other programming languages like C, Java, etc. If,

for instance, you've accidentally put a semicolon in the middle of a statement, JavaScript would see the statement as incomplete and produce an error for it.

3. Misusing the quotation marks - quotation marks tell the interpreter that you're using a string, so if you enclose a variable or a number in quotation marks, you're effectively turning them into strings. This'll lead to anomalies when you try to perform numerical operations onto numbers that you've accidentally enclosed in quotation marks.

So far, these are only the most common mistakes newbies tend to make, but along the way you should be able to see bugs and errors quite easily as you get more practice making more complex codes.

Recap

We've covered quite a lot of concepts so far, so let's review what we've learned:

1. Variables and data types

○ *numbers - can be integers or numbers that contain decimals (e.g., 3.14, 5, 100)*

○ *strings - anything you enclose in quotation marks (e.g., "5", "I am a JavaScript master", "I love the number 7")*

○ *booleans - true or false*

In order to declare a variable, simply type:

```
var <variable name> = <value>;
```

You can also just declare the variable name without the value if you don't have one yet:

```
var <variable name>;
```

JavaScript doesn't care what type of data you put in. If you've programmed in C or Java, you might have been used to declaring the variable's data type (int, float, char, etc.), but in JavaScript, you can put anything in a variable without any problems.

2. Pop-up boxes

○ *alert("Hi There!") - you can pop-up alerts to the user.*

o   *confirm("Are you sure?") - you can ask for a confirmation from the user.*

o   *prompt("Type anything here.") - you can ask for input from the user*

3. Flow-control

o   *if-else statement - in a nutshell, if the first condition is met, then do whatever's in the first bracket enclosure and skip the 'else' part. Otherwise, go to the bracket enclosure for the 'else' condition and do whatever's inside it.*

Chapter 14. Regular Expressions

What are regular expressions?

Regular expressions represent a pattern. In JavaScript, regular expressions can be used to perform operations such as searching a pattern, replacing a pattern, checking if a string matches a given pattern or breaking of a string into smaller strings based on a specific pattern. In JavaScript, regular expressions are objects.

Making a regular expression

There are two ways by which you can create regular expressions in JavaScript, which are:

- **Using regular expression literal:**
  In this method, the pattern is specified within two slashes // followed by the character(s) which are known as modifiers. You will learn about what modifiers are later in this chapter; modifiers are optional.
  Syntax:

/pattern/modifiers

/pattern/

If this method is used, then the regular expression is compiled when the script is loaded and thus if the regular expression is constant, this method improves the performance of the program.

- **Using constructor of RegExp object:**

  In this method, we use the 'new' keyword to initialize a new object of RegExp which stands for Regular Expression. The pattern is passed as the first argument to the RegExp constructor and the modifier as the second argument, note that the modifier argument here is optional too.

  Syntax:

new RegExp("pattern", "modifiers");

new RegExp("pattern");

If this method is used, then the regular expression is compiled at runtime, this method is generally used where regular expression is not a constant.

MODIFIERS

A modifier is used to change the way a match of pattern based on regular expression is done. Listed below are the modifiers and the details on how they affect the operation.

- **i**

  Makes the match case insensitive, by default matching done is with regular expressions is case sensitive.

- **m**

  Makes the match of pattern extend to multiple lines one if there are more than one lines in the string that the match is being performed on.

- **g**

By default, the operation stops after finding the first match for the pattern, but if this modifier is used the operations don't stop at the first match and thus performs a 'g'lobal match.

Simple patterns

If you want to match a sequence of character directly, then you can write it in the place of the pattern. For example, the regular expression /test/ will match any string with 'test' in it, so there would be a match for a string like 'this is a test, ' but there would not be any match for string like 'this is a est' because the character 't' is missing from the sequence specified.

Certain characters denotes something special in a regular expression like '*' or '.', if you want to match these characters directly then you need to escape them, i.e., add a backslash before them. So for matching the exact string 'te*st', the regular expression will be /te*st/. You will learn about all the characters with a special significance in regular expressions in the very next section.

Special character(s)

Here is a list of special character(s) that can be used for a regular expression and what they do:

- ^

    If present at the start of the regular expression, this character signifies that the following pattern should be matched from the beginning of the input. If the 'm' modifier is used, then the starting of each line is also tested for the match. For example, the regular expression /^test/ will not match anything in the string 'this is a test' as 'test' is not present at the beginning of the string, but the same regular expression will match with the string 'test is going on'.

- $

    If present at the end of the regular expression, this character signifies that the pattern should be matched with the end of the line. If the 'm' modifier is used then the end of each line is tested for the match.

For example, the regular expression /test$/ will not match anything in the string 'test is going on' as 'test' is not present at the end of the string, but the same regular expression will match the string 'this is a test.'

- *

This character is used to match the expression preceding this character zero or more times.

For example, the regular expression /te*st/ will match 't' followed by zero or more 'e' and that followed by 'st', so the string 'this is a teeeeeest' as well as the string 'this is a tst' will be matched but the string 'this is teees' won't be matched since a 't' is missing from the sequence to be matched.

- +

This character is used to match the expression preceding this character one or more times, i.e., if the preceding expression occurs at-least once. For example, the regular expression /te*st/ will match the string 'this is a teeeeeest' but won't match the string 'this is a tst' or the string 'this is a tees'.

- **?**

  This character is used to match the expression preceding this character zero or one time.

  For example, the regular expression /te?st/ will match the string 'this is a test' and 'this is a tst' but won't match the string 'this is a teest' or the string 'this is a tes'.

- **{x}**

  This form of expression is used to match exactly x occurrences of the preceding expression, where x is a positive integer.

  For example, the regular expression /te{3}st/ will match the string 'this is a teeest' but won't match the string 'this is a test' or the string 'this is a teeeeest'.

- **{x, y}**

  This form of expression is used to match any number of occurrences between x and y of the preceding expression, where x and y both are positive integers and x is less than or equal to y.

  For example, the regular expression /te{3, 6}st/ will match the string 'this is a teeest' and 'this is a teeeeest' but won't match the string 'this is a test' or the string 'this is a teeeeeeest'.

- **{x,}**

  This form of expression is used to match at-least x occurrences of the preceding expression, where x is a positive integer.

  For example, the regular expression /te{3,}st/ will match the string 'this is a teeest' but won't match the string 'this is a test' or the string 'this is a teest'.

- **.**

  This character is used to match any character except a newline one.

  For example, the regular expression /te.st/ will match the string 'this is a tOst' and 'this is a tZst' but won't match the string 'this is a tst'.

- **[abc]**

  This form of expression is used to match any character or expression that is present between the square brackets.

  For example, the regular expression /t[eyz]st/ will match the string 'this is a test' and 'this is a tzst' but won't match the string 'this is a tpst' or the string 'this is a trst'.

  You can use ranges like a-z and 0-9 which matches all the character from 'a' to 'z' and '0' to '9' respectively.For example, the regular expression /t[a-z]st/ will match the string 'this is a test' and 'this is a tkst' but won't match the string 'this is a t9st' or the string 'this is a t2st', but the regular expression /t[a-z0-9]st/ will match all the strings mentioned in this particular example.

- **[^abc]**

This form of expression is used to match anything EXCEPT the character(s) or expression(s) that is present between the [^ and].

For example, the regular expression /t[^eyz]st/ will match the string 'this is a tpst' and 'this is a trst' but won't match the string 'this is a test' or the string 'this is a tyst'.

You can use the ranges, just like in the above-mentioned expression, in this form of expression too.For example, the regular expression /t[^a-z]st/ will match the string 'this is a t9st' and 'this is a t8st' but won't match the string 'this is a test' or the string 'this is a tast'.

- **(abc)**

This form of expression is called a capture group. The pattern between the () is matched normally but is stored in memory for later use; you will learn about this expression usage in methods like .exec() later in this chapter.

Meta Characters

These are the special character sequences that are used to match certain characters or range of characters. Some of the most used metacharacters are:

- \w

  Matches any word character, i.e., any alphanumeric character including underscore.

- \W

  Matches any non-word character. All the characters that are not matched by \w are matched by this.

- \d

  Matches any digit, i.e., any character from 0 to 9.

- \D

  Matches any non-digit, i.e., any character except from 0 to 9.

- \w

  Matches any whitespace character, i.e., characters like tab, space, line ends etc.

- \W

Matches any non-whitespace character, i.e., any character except whitespace characters like tab, space, line ends, etc.

Using regular expressions

Now that you have learned about how to make up a regular expression, we can move on to learn about how to put them into action. Listed below are the methods which you can use with a regular expression.

- **regexObject.test(string)**

  This method tries to match the regular expression with the string passed as the argument, if it is matched, this method returns true else false.

  Examples:

var result1 = /example/.test('this is an example');

var result2 = /example/.test('what is this');

console.log(result1); //prints 'true' on the console screen

cosnole.log(result2);//prints 'false' on the console screen

- **regexObject.exec(string)**

  This method tries to match the regular expression with the string passed as the argument, if it is matched, this method returns an array filled with information else it returns null. The returned array first item is the matched string and the second is the first capture group present if any and third item is the second capture group present if any and so on.

  Examples:

var result1 = /exam(pl)e/.test('this is an example');

var result2 = /example/.test('what is this');

console.log(result1[0]); //prints 'example' on the console screen

console.log(result[1]); //prints 'pl' on the console screen

cosnole.log(result2); //prints 'null' on the console screen

- **string.search(regex)**

  This method tries to find a match of the regex passed as the argument. If found, it returns the index(position) of the match else returns -1.

Note that the index begins from 0, not from 1. So the first character's index in a string is 0 and the second character's index is 1.

Examples:

```
var result1 = 'an example'.search(/a.p/);

var result2 = 'an example'.search(/55/);

console.log( result ); //prints '5' on the console screen

cosnole.log( result2 ); //prints '-1' on the console screen
```

- string.replace(regex, replacer)

This method tries to find a match of regex passed as the first argument if found it replaces the match with the second argument(replacer).
Example:

```
var original = "this is an example";

//replcaes first s and a with 9

var new = original.replace(/[sa]/, '9');

//replcaes each s and a with 9, since the'g' modifier is used

var new2 = original.replace(/[sa]/g, '9');
```

console.log(new);//prints 'thi9 is an example' on the console screen

console.log(new2);//prints 'thi9 i9 9n ex9mple' on the console screen

> We can also use capture groups in the regular expression in this function and then use them in the replacer string. If in the replacer string we use a $ sign followed by a number then that $ sign with the number is replaced by the capture group of that index. For example, $1 gets replaced by the first capture group in the regular expression and $2 by the second one and so on. Example:

var original = "this is an example";

//places _ on both side of each s and a

var new = original.replace(/([sa])/g, '_$1_');

console.log(new);//prints 'thi_s_ i_s_ _a_n ex_a_mple' on the console screen

In this chapter, you have learned about regular expressions. I hope you have got a basic idea of regular expressions in JavaScript after reading this chapter.

Hoisting

What is hoisting?

The word hoist means to lift or raise up by means of some mechanical device like a pulley, but in JavaScript, hoisting means that the functions and variable declarations are moved to the top of the scope or context they are declared in, i.e., lifted up as in hoist, thus the word 'hoist'ing.

The declarations aren't really moved to the top, they are just put first into the compiled code.

Variable hoisting

For example the following code:

```
x = 21;

console.log( x );

var x;
```

Really compiles as this:

```
var x;

x = 21;

console.log(x);
```

As you can see the declaration has moved to the top of the current context, this is what hoisting is.

Let's understand this with a more suitable example:

console.log(x); // prints 'undefined' on the console screen

console.log(y); // throws a ReferenceError saying 'y is not defined'

var x;

This happens because 'x' being declared in the current context, though it is below the console.log line, it is moved at the top of the context and as there is no assignment done to 'x', it is set to 'undefined' by default, whereas in case of 'y' it is not available anywhere in current context, therefore, a ReferenceError is thrown.

Note that the assignment operation is not hoisted, only the declaration is.

Example:

console.log(x); //prints 'undefined' on the console screen

var x; // only this statement is hoisted

x = 21; // this is not

You must be wondering about, what if we assign the value to variable while declaring it, like 'var x = 21;', though here it seems that you are assigning value to variable while declaring it but in fact internally the variable is first declared and then the value is assigned to it, so it is equivalent to 'var x; x = 21;'. So if you declare a variable like this below the line where it is being used but in the same context then only declaration part is hoisted.

Example:

> console.log(x); //prints 'undefined' on the console screen
>
> var x = 21;

This is how the above code is compiled:

> var x;
>
> console.log(x); //prints 'undefined' on the console screen

x = 21;

Function hoisting

Just as variable hoisting, functions are also hoisted. As a result the functions can be called even before they are declared, given that it is declared in the current context or scope.

Example:

> test();

```
function test() {

console.log('This is a test');

}
```

//prints 'This is a test' on the console screen

It is to be noted that function expressions, i.e., functions that are assigned to variables through the assignment operator '=' are not hoisted. The case of hoisting function expression is same as assigning a value a variable, which has been discussed above.

Example:

Just as variable

test(); // throws a TypeError saying 'test is not a function'

testRandom(); // throws ReferenceError saying 'testRandom is not defined'

var test = function {

console.log('This is a test');

};

In the above example, the difference in types of error is caused due to hoisting. As visible the variable 'test' is declared in the current scope therefore its declaration is moved at top and hence it is declared, though its value is undefined at the point where it is used, so a TypeError is thrown which indicates that the 'test' is defined but is not a function, whereas the function 'testRandom' is not declared anywhere, so a ReferenceError is thrown.

Order of precedence of hoisting

Functions are always hoisted over variable declaration.

Example:

<u>function test() {</u>

<u>//function code</u>

}

var test;

<u>console.log(typeof test); //prints 'function' on the</u>
<u>console screen</u>

Even if the position of the variable line and function line are swapped in the above example, the output will remain the same.

But functions are not hoisted over variable declaration, given the assignment is done above the line where it is being used.

Example:

<u>function test() {</u>

```
//function code
}
```

```
var test = 21; //now assignment is being done too
console.log( typeof test ); //prints 'number' on the
console screen
```

Even if the position of the variable line and function line are swapped in the above example, the output will remain the same.

As mentioned this is valid as long as the assignment is done above the line where it is being used, when the assignment is done below, then the function is hoisted over the assignment.

Example:

```
function test() {
//function code
}
```

```
var test;
console.log(typeof test);//prints 'function' on the
console screen
test = 21;
console.log(typeof test);//prints 'number' on the
console screen
```

CONCLUSION

It is always the best practice to declare variables or functions on the top of the scope where they will be used to avoid any confusion, even though due to hoisting variable declaration will be moved to the top of the scope or context automatically.

Chapter 15. Basic Data Types of Variables

Variables have four basic data types. These are numbers, strings, Boolean, and objects. We'll skim through these types, because going in-depth in discussing them will leave us not time in learning your JavaScript basic codes.

1. Numbers

In JavaScript, generally, all numbers are considered as 64-bit floating point numbers. When there are no values after the decimal point, the number is presented as a whole number.

Examples:

- 9.000 is presented as 9

- 6.000 is presented as 6

- 2.00 is presented as 2

JavaScript and other computer programming languages are based on the IEEE 754 standard, or the Standard for Floating-Point Arithmetic.

Number literals can be a floating-point number, an integer or a hexadecimal.

Example of floating-point numbers:

- 4.516

- 9.134

- 6.01

- 4.121

Examples of integers:

- 34

- 45

- 21

- 30

Examples of hexadecimal numbers

- **OxFF**

- **-OxCCFF**

Special number values

- **'NAN' AND 'INFINITY' - are JavaScript's two 'error values'**

The NaN (Not a Number) error appears when the browser cannot parse the number, or when an operation failed.

On the other hand, Infinity is an error that appears when the number cannot be represented because of its magnitude. The error also appears when you divide a number by zero (0).

- **-0 AND +0 – the -0 rarely appears, so don't get confused about these special number values. You can ignore them, for now.**

- **NULL – these are obtained when the browser cannot return a value.**

2. Strings

Strings are data types that are typically enclosed in matching single quotes or double quotes. The elements can be numbers or texts.

3. Boolean

These data types represent either 'true' or 'false'. Through the use of Boolean, you can find out whether a JavaScript expression is 'true' or 'false'.

The 'true' returns are generally obtained from expressions with true values, such as number equations and similar expressions.

In contrast, 'false' returns are obtained from expressions without true values.

EXAMPLE 1:

(3 > 9)

Of course, this is false because 9 is definitely greater than 3.

Example 2:

(2<3)

Obviously, the statement is 'true'. There's no need for an explanation on that one.

EXAMPLE 3:

(4=9)

A 'ReferenceError' will occurre on the third example. This is because in JavaScript language, and most computer programming language, the equal sign (=) is not a symbol of equality. The equal sign is used in assigning the values or elements of variables.

See next image:

When the correct JavaScript syntax was utilized, the expression returned with a 'false' value because even with the correct sign, 4 is still not equal to 9.

4. Objects

Objects encompass all data types in the sense that numbers, Booleans, and strings can be objects. Data, such as arrays, regular expressions, dates and math are objects, as well

Objects contain many values and have properties (name:values pair) and methods (process or action). Thus, they are containers of named values. This name:values pair is called property (name) and property values (values).

They can be a collection of various different data.

EXAMPLES:

- student: "Johnson"

- country: "Sweden"

- street: "Reed Avenue"

EXAMPLE:

```
var students =
{firstName: "Lena", lastName: "Dean"};
```

SEE IMAGE BELOW:

They are typically expressed in pairs as 'name:value'. Take note of the colon in between the pair, and the commas after each pair. The property values are in quotes, and the entire statement is in brackets.

Chapter 16. The window object

What is the 'window' object?

As the name suggests, this object represents the current window. All major parts of the BOM are the direct children of this object. For example, window.document (The DOM), window.history, etc. Note that each tab on the browser has a unique window object. They don't share the same object! Some properties like window size, which is the same in all tabs, have the same value and technically those properties are shared. The window object contains references to useful properties and functions that may not strictly be related to the window only.

Even though there is no strict standard for the 'window' object, it is supported by all browsers.

The default references to the 'window' object

Since the 'window' object is present on top of hierarchy with no other object present at its level, all references to the window object's methods and properties can be made without writing the starting of the dotted notation part, i.e., the 'window.' part. Example:

WINDOW.ALERT()

alert()// same as above

var x = window.length;

var y = length;

// x will be equal to y since the refer to the same property

All variables declared are actually 'window' object's properties

As stated above, even the variables declared in the program are the direct child of the 'window' object, and are its properties.

Example:

var x = 21;

console.log(window.x); // prints '21' on the console screen

The 'window' object's method references

Here is the list of the 'window' object's major methods and their description:

- .ALERT("MESSAGE")

This method is used to display a dialog box on the screen, a type of pop-up, with a message that is passed as the argument of this function. The dialog box this will open has only one button, which is "OK"

Example:

window.alert(" Hello from JavaScript! ")

OR

alert(" Hello from JavaScript! ")

Both of the above statements are equivalent.

- .CONFIRM("MESSAGE")

This method is used to display a dialog box on the screen, with a message that is passed as the argument of this function, along with two buttons which are "OK" and "Cancel". This method returns a boolean value. It returns true if the "OK" button was clicked and false if the "Cancel" button was clicked.

Example:

var val = confirm(" Do you accept our terms and agreement? ");

if(val == true) console.log("User pressed OK");

else console.log("User pressed Cancel");

- **.prompt("message", "default text")**

This method is used to display a dialog box on the screen, with a message and an input box where the user can enter a value, along with the "OK" and "Cancel" button. This method is used to take an input from the user. The 'default text' parameter is the default value of the input box in the dialog box. This method returns the value entered by the user in the input box if the user presses the "OK" button. If the user presses the "Cancel" button, this method returns 'null'.

Example:

var val = prompt("What is your name?", "Enter your name here");

if(val === null) console.log("User pressed the cancel button");

else console.log("User's name is " + val);

- **.open([URL,] [name,] [specs,] [replace])**

This method is used to open a new window. All the parameters in this method are optional. This method returns the window object of the newly created window. Here is the description of the parameters:

→ URL

This parameter is used to specify the URL of the page to be opened in the new window. The default value of this parameter is 'about:blank' which opens a window with a blank page.

→   NAME

This parameter is used to specify how the URL is opened in the window or the name of the window. The following values are used as this parameter:

❖   **'_blank'**: This is the default value of the 'name' parameter. If this value is used, the URL is loaded in a new window.

❖   **'_parent'**: If this value is used, the URL is loaded in the parent frame.

❖   **'_top'**:   If this value is used, the URL replaces any of the framesets that have been loaded previously.

❖   **'_self'**: If this value is used, the URL replaces the current page and is loaded in the current page.

❖   **Any other value**: If any other value is used, it acts as the name of the window. Note that the name of the window is not the same as the title of the window.

→   SPECS

This parameter is a string which contains some attributes, separated by a comma, of the new window to be opened. You can specify things such as width, height etc. of the new window using this parameter.

➔ REPLACE

This parameter specifies whether the new URL to be opened will replace the current URL in the history object list or not. It takes boolean values, true or false. If 'true' is passed as the value of this parameter, the new URL replaces the current URL in the history object list. If 'false' is passed, it does not.

Example:

var newWindow = window.open("http://mySite.com", "", "height=210,width=700"); // creates a new window with 210px height and 700px width.

- .CLOSE()

This method is used to close a window.

Example:

var newWindow = window.open("http://mySite.com"); newWindow.close(); // closes the window as soon as it opens

- **.scrollTo(xCoords, yCoords)**

This method is used to set the scroll of the window to the specified coordinates in the document.

- **.resizeTo(height, width)**

This method is used to resize the window to a specified height and width. The height and width passed as the parameters in this argument are in pixels(px).

The 'window' object's properties
Here is the list of the 'window' object's major properties and their description:

- .PAGEXOFFSET

This property returns the current horizontal scroll distance in pixels(px). It is basically the **horizontal** distance between the actual left corner of the page and the current window left corner.

- .SCROLLX

Same as the window.pageXOffset property.

- .PAGEYOFFSET

This property returns the current vertical scroll distance in pixels(px). It is basically the **vertical** distance between the actual left corner of the page and the current window left corner.

- .SCROLLY

Same as the window.pageYOffset property.

- .OUTERHEIGHT

This property returns the full height of the window, including the document, the toolbar, and the scrollbar.

- .OUTERWIDTH

This property returns the full width of the window, including the document, the toolbar, and the scrollbar.

- .INNERHEIGHT

This property returns the height of the content area of the window where the HTML document is displayed. It does **not** include the scrollbar or toolbar height.

- .INNERWIDTH

This property returns the width of the content area of the window where the HTML document is displayed. It does **not** include the scrollbar or toolbar height.

- .FRAMES

Returns an array of all the <iframe> element's in the current window if any.

Example:

<u>\<body></u>

<iframe src="https://mySite1.com"></iframe>

<iframe src="https://mySite2.com"></iframe>

<SCRIPT>

console.log(window.frames.length); // prints '2' on the console screen
</SCRIPT>

</body>

- .CLOSED

Returns a boolean value indicating whether a window has been closed or not. If the returned value is true, the window has been closed. If false, the window has not been closed.

Example:

var newWindow = window.open("http://mySite.com");

function isNewWindowOpen()

{

if(newWindow.closed == true)return "NO";

else return "YES";

}

Chapter 17. Maps and Sets

The map class is used to hold a set of key value pairs. The values can be primitive types (like numbers or strings) or object types. The syntax for declaring the map object is shown below.

```
var mapname=new Map();
```

Where 'mapname' is the name of the new map object. To add a key value pair to the Map, you can use the 'set' method as shown below.

mapname.set(key,value)

Where 'key' is the key for the key value pair and 'value' is the subsequent value for the key. To get a value from the map, we can use the 'get' method to get the value for the subsequent key. Let's look at a way maps can be used through an example.

Example 64: The following program is used to showcase how to use a map class in JavaScript.

The following things need to be noted about the above program:

- We first declare a map object by using the 'new' clause and using the 'map' class.

- Next we set a key/value pair by using the 'set' method.

- Finally we display the value for the key by using the 'get' method.

With this program, the output is as follows:

JavaScript Program

The value for key1 is value1

Let's look at another example of using maps, this time using multiple keys and values.

Example 65: The following program shows how to use a map class with multiple key value pairs.

```html
<!DOCTYPE html>

<html>

<body>

 <h2>JavaScript Program</h2>

  <p id="demo1"></p>

  <p id="demo2"></p>
```

```
    <p id="demo3"></p>

<script>

var map=new Map();

map.set("key1","value1");

map.set("key2","value2");

map.set("key3","value3");

document.getElementById("demo1").innerHTML   =
"The value for key1 is "+map.get("key1");

document.getElementById("demo2").innerHTML   =
"The value for key2 is "+map.get("key2");

document.getElementById("demo3").innerHTML   =
"The value for key3 is "+map.get("key3");

</script>

</body>

</html>
```

With this program, the output is as follows:

JavaScript Program

The value for key1 is value1

The value for key2 is value2

The value for key3 is value3

There are multiple methods available for the map class. Let's look at them in more detail.

Table 3: Map Properties and Methods

Property	Description
size	This is used to display the number of elements in the map
clear	This is used to clear all the elements in the map
delete	This is used to delete an element in the map
has	This is used to check if a map has a particular element or not
keys	This is used to get the keys of the map collection
values	This is used to get the values of the map collection

size Property

The 'size' property is used to display the number of elements in the map. Let's now look at an example of this property.

Example 66: The following program is used to showcase how to use the size property.

```
<!DOCTYPE html>

<html>

<body>

  <h2>JavaScript Program</h2>

    <p id="demo1"></p>

<script>

var map=new Map();

map.set("key1","value1");

map.set("key2","value2");

map.set("key3","value3");

document.getElementById("demo1").innerHTML    =
"The number of elements in the map "+map.size;
```

```
</script>

</body>

</html>
```

With this program, the output is as follows:

JavaScript Program

The number of elements in the map 3

clear Method

The 'clear' method is used to clear all the elements in the map. Let's now look at an example of this method.

Example 67: The following program is used to showcase how to use the clear method.

```
<!DOCTYPE html>

<html>

<body>

  <h2>JavaScript Program</h2>

    <p id="demo1"></p>

    <p id="demo2"></p>
```

```
<script>

var map=new Map();

map.set("key1","value1");

map.set("key2","value2");

map.set("key3","value3");

document.getElementById("demo1").innerHTML    =
"The number of elements in the map "+map.size;

map.clear();

document.getElementById("demo2").innerHTML    =
"The number of elements in the map "+map.size;

</script>

</body>

</html>
```

With this program, the output is as follows:

JavaScript Program

The number of elements in the map 3
The number of elements in the map 0

delete Method

The 'delete' method is used to delete an element in the map. Let's now look at an example of this method.

Example 68: The following program is used to showcase how to use the delete method.

```
<!DOCTYPE html>
<html>
<body>

  <h2>JavaScript Program</h2>

    <p id="demo1"></p>

    <p id="demo2"></p>
<script>
var map=new Map();
map.set("key1","value1");
map.set("key2","value2");
map.set("key3","value3");
```

```
document.getElementById("demo1").innerHTML    =
"The number of elements in the map "+map.size;

map.delete("key2");

document.getElementById("demo2").innerHTML    =
"The number of elements in the map "+map.size;

</script>

</body>

</html>
```

With this program, the output is as follows:

JavaScript Program

The number of elements in the map 3

The number of elements in the map 2

has Method

The 'has' method is used to check if a map has a particular element or not. Let's now look at an example of this method.

Example 69: The following program is used to showcase how to use the has method.

```html
<!DOCTYPE html>
<html>
<body>

  <h2>JavaScript Program</h2>

    <p id="demo1"></p>

    <p id="demo2"></p>

<script>

var map=new Map();

map.set("key1","value1");

map.set("key2","value2");

map.set("key3","value3");

document.getElementById("demo1").innerHTML   =
"The number of elements in the map "+map.size;

document.getElementById("demo2").innerHTML   =
"Does  the  map  have  the  element  key2  "
+map.has("key2");

</script>

</body>

</html>
```

With this program, the output is as follows:

JavaScript Program

The number of elements in the map 3

Does the map have the element key2 true

keys Method

The 'keys' method is used to acquire the keys of the map collection. Let's now look at an example of this method.

Example 70: The following program is used to showcase how to use the keys method.

```
<!DOCTYPE html>

<html>

<body>

  <h2>JavaScript Program</h2>

    <p id="demo1"></p>

<script>

var map=new Map();

map.set("key1","value1");

map.set("key2","value2");
```

```javascript
map.set("key3","value3");

var text="";

for (var key of map.keys())

  {

    text+=key;

    text+="</br>";

  }

document.getElementById("demo1").innerHTML    =
text;
</script>
</body>
</html>
```

With this program, the output is as follows:

<u>JavaScript Program</u>

key1

key2

key3

<u>values Method</u>

The 'values' method is used to get the values of the map collection. Let's now look at an example of this method.

Example 71: The following program is used to showcase how to use the values method.

```
<!DOCTYPE html>

<html>

<body>

  <h2>JavaScript Program</h2>

    <p id="demo1"></p>

<script>

var map=new Map();

map.set("key1","value1");

map.set("key2","value2");

map.set("key3","value3");

var text="";

for (var value of map.values())
```

```
{

  text+= value;

  text+="</br>";

}

document.getElementById("demo1").innerHTML   =
text;

</script>

</body>

</html>
```

With this program, the output is as follows:

JavaScript Program

    value1

    value2

    value3

set Class

The 'set' class lets you store unique values of any type. The values can be primitive types, such as numbers and strings, or object types. The syntax for declaring the 'set' object is shown below.

```
var setname=new Set();
```

Where 'setname' is the name of the new set object. To add a value to the set, you can use the 'add' method as shown below.

```
setname.add(value)
```

To check whether the set has a value we can use the 'has' method. Let's look at a way sets can be used through an example.

Example 72: The following program is used to showcase how to use a set class in JavaScript.

```
<!DOCTYPE html>

<html>

<body>

  <h2>JavaScript Program</h2>

    <p id="demo1"></p>

<script>

var set=new Set();
```

```
set.add("value1");

set.add("value2");

set.add("value3");

var text="";

document.getElementById("demo1").innerHTML    =
"Does the set contain value2 "+set.has("value2");

</script>

</body>

</html>
```

With this program, the output is as follows:

JavaScript Program

Does the set contain value2 true

Table 4: Set Properties and Methods

Property	Description
size	**This is used to display the number of elements in the set**
clear	**This is used to clear all the elements in the map**

delete	This is used to delete an element in the map
values	This is used to get the values of the map collection

size Property

The 'size' property is used to display the number of elements in the set. Let's look at an example of this property.

Example 73: The following program is used to showcase how to use the size property.

```
<!DOCTYPE html>

<html>

<body>

  <h2>JavaScript Program</h2>

    <p id="demo1"></p>

<script>

var set=new Set();

set.add("value1");
```

```
set.add("value2");

set.add("value3");

var text="";

document.getElementById("demo1").innerHTML    =
"The number of elements is "+ set.size;

</script>

</body>

</html>
```

With this program, the output is as follows:

JavaScript Program

The number of elements is 3

clear Method

The 'clear' method is used to clear all the elements in the set. Let's now look at an example of this method.

Example 74: The following program is used to showcase how to use the clear method.

```html
<!DOCTYPE html>
<html>
<body>

  <h2>JavaScript Program</h2>

    <p id="demo1"></p>

    <p id="demo2"></p>
<script>
var set=new Set();

set.add("value1");

set.add("value2");

set.add("value3");

document.getElementById("demo1").innerHTML   =
"The number of elements is "+ set.size;

set.clear();

document.getElementById("demo2").innerHTML   =
"The number of elements is "+ set.size;

</script>
</body>
</html>
```

With this program, the output is as follows:

JavaScript Program

The number of elements is 3

The number of elements is 0

9.10 delete Method

The 'delete' method is used to delete an element in the set. Let's now look at an example of this method.

Example 75: The following program is used to showcase how to use the delete method.

```
<!DOCTYPE html>
<html>
<body>

  <h2>JavaScript Program</h2>

    <p id="demo1"></p>

    <p id="demo2"></p>
<script>

var set=new Set();

set.add("value1");
```

```
set.add("value2");

set.add("value3");

document.getElementById("demo1").innerHTML    =
"The number of elements is "+ set.size;

set.delete("value2");

document.getElementById("demo2").innerHTML    =
"The number of elements is "+ set.size;

</script>

</body>

</html>
```

With this program, the output is as follows:

JavaScript Program

The number of elements is 3

The number of elements is 2

9.11 values Method

The 'values' method is used to get the values of the set collection. Let's quickly look at an example of this method.

Example 76: The following program is used to showcase how to use the values method.

```html
<!DOCTYPE html>

<html>

<body>

  <h2>JavaScript Program</h2>

    <p id="demo1"></p>

<script>

var set=new Set();

set.add("value1");

set.add("value2");

set.add("value3");

var text="";

for (var value of set.values())

  {

    text+=value;

    text+="</br>";

  }
```

```
document.getElementById("demo1").innerHTML    =
text;

</script>

</body>

</html>
```

With this program, the output is as follows:

JavaScript Program

value1

value2

value3

Conclusion

In this book, I have provided you with the basic knowledge that you will need to start your journey in programming using JavaScript. The different concepts taught here, such as functions, loops, branches, and objects will equip you with the skills that you need to create your first JavaScript project.

Also, continue practicing and taking on small projects to start improving your skills. Through the knowledge imparted in this book, coupled with practice, you will be able to work on building your own websites or coding your own projects.

In your further study, I recommend that you learn and take on advanced topics such as troubleshooting in JavaScript, explore different frameworks and libraries, and expand your knowledge in using regular expressions.

I would also strongly recommend that you learn other programming languages, so that you may be able to take your knowledge to the next level, and become a top-class programmer. Because you have gone through this course, you will be astonished to find that learning other languages is easier than expected, for JavaScript has strikingly paved the way for you. I recommend Python or Java as the best languages to learn next.